When Someone You Love

Is Wiccan

A Guide
to Witchcraft and
Paganism for Concerned
Friends, Nervous Parents,
and Curious Co-workers

Carl McColman

NEW PAGE BOOKS
A division of The Career Press, Inc.
Franklin Lakes, NJ

WHEN SOMEONE YOU LOVE IS WICCAN
EDITED BY NICOLE DeFELICE
TYPESET BY EILEEN DOW MUNSON
Cover design by Jean William Naumann
Printed in the U.S.A. by Book-mart Press

To order this title, please call toll-free 1-800-CAREER-1 (NJ and Canada: 201-848-0310) to order using VISA or MasterCard, or for further information on books from Career Press.

The Career Press, Inc., 3 Tice Road, PO Box 687,
Franklin Lakes, NJ 07417
www.careerpress.com
www.newpagebooks.com

Library of Congress Cataloging-in-Publication Data

McColman, Carl.
    When someone you love is Wiccan : a guide to witchcraft and paganism for concerned friends, nervous parents, and curious co-workers / by Carl McColman.
        p. cm.
    Includes index.
    ISBN 1-56414-622-7 (pbk.)
        1. Witchcraft. 2. Paganism. I. Title.

BF1566 .M36 2003
299—dc21

2002026408

Dedication

For Meg Anderson, John Beasley, and Susan Strauss—three dear friends, each of whom embodies a spirit of love and honor that transcends all religious bounds.

Acknowledgments

Thanks to the many people who supported the process of writing this book, including Linda Roghaar; Mike Lewis and everyone at New Page; Candace Apple and everyone at the Phoenix and Dragon Bookstore; the members of the Earth Mystic community and the Atlanta Pagan community; all my students; and most of all, my wife, Fran McColman, and stepdaughter, Rhiannon Wilburn. Thanks also to my family and non-Pagan friends, for giving me opportunities to express some of the ideas presented in this book.

Contents

Part Nine: Practical Considerations 181

Introduction

Dear Reader,

Thank you for picking up *When Someone You Love Is Wiccan*. It is my hope that this little book will help you to understand someone close to you—perhaps your son or daughter, or some other relative; perhaps a friend, neighbor, or co-worker. Whoever this person is, he or she is interested in or participates in a beautiful, but often misunderstood, spiritual tradition. This tradition is known by a number of different names, including Paganism, nature spirituality, Goddess spirituality, and Wicca. It's also known as the old religion or the craft. It is actually new religion, but it draws its inspiration, at least in part, from a subject shrouded in mystery: Witchcraft.

Now you are wondering just what Paganism or Wicca is all about. I hope this book will help you to understand and appreciate this special form of spirituality.

Perhaps you're uncomfortable with the mere idea of Paganism. Perhaps you're asking yourself, "How could my child/friend/co-worker have gotten involved with this?" Or maybe you prefer not to think about it at all. Maybe you secretly hope that some day you'll be talking on the phone with the Wiccan in your life, and he or she will say, "Oh by the way, I found a nice little Christian church that I have been attending, and I'm thinking about joining." Or maybe you've accepted that, while Paganism is not your choice for religion and spirituality, you respect the right of each person to make his or her own spiritual choice. In any event, I believe knowledge is a powerful tool to help people get along better in this crazy world we live in. So I hope the information in this book will help you to be more informed about the Pagan path.

Paganism, Wicca, and Witchcraft all mean slightly different things, just like Lutheran and Methodist and Baptist refer to different forms of Christianity. But just as these churches are all part of Christianity, so is Paganism, Wicca, and Witchcraft all part of a worldwide movement of spirituality and religion that is based in reverence for nature. That's why it's called "Nature Spirituality." This movement believes that Mother Nature, or Mother Earth, is actually as much a part of God as is God the Father. Pagans think of Mother Nature as a Goddess, so this religion is also called Goddess Spirituality. It is a new religious movement, but is based on ancient spiritual practices from around the world. Nature spirituality is not a cult, and Pagans do not worship the devil. In fact, Pagans don't even believe in the devil.

If you are a religious person, I'm sure your faith means a lot to you. Perhaps you are an active member of your church, and you raised your children in the faith. Even though Paganism and Wicca may seem strange and unusual to you, I hope you'll see that Pagans are just as devoted and committed to the highest principles of nature spirituality as other people are to their faiths, whether Christian, Jewish, Muslim, or whatever. The Pagan path may not be the same as yours, but Pagans walk it with a similar sense of commitment, integrity, and responsibility. For Wiccans and Pagans, their path is about becoming a better person and working for the healing of our natural environment and our society.

It may be difficult for you to accept that someone you love is a Witch. After all, in our society, Witches are often thought to be bad people, malevolent evil-doers who curse and poison their enemies. Look at the Wicked Witch in *The Wizard of Oz*, for example. Of course, Pagans believe these stereotypes are inaccurate and unfair, based on centuries of misunderstanding. But it is understandable if the word "Witch" makes you uncomfortable.

If the Pagan you know is your child, it may bother you that he or she does not participate in your religion. This can be especially difficult for conservative Christians.

Some Christians say that if you merely dabble in non-Christian religion, then you have sinned against God and are going to go to hell. Perhaps you're afraid that a Pagan's eternal soul may be in danger. And then there's the influence of modern science that often looks at spirituality and mysticism with skepticism and disdain. Of course, modern science is just as dismissive of Christianity as it is of Witchcraft, but at least Christians don't seem as "kooky" as Witches. Maybe you think that Pagans are either spiritually deluded, or else have gotten caught up in something silly and irrational. But either way, it looks bad to you.

I honor and respect your concern. I've been studying modern Paganism since 1983, and have actually practiced the Pagan path since 1990. In other words, I spent seven years thinking about and researching Wicca and other forms of Paganism before I took the step of actually living a Pagan life. Let me share with you some of the things that I learned in the years I spent researching Paganism and Witchcraft.

✪ Paganism (or "Neopaganism," which means the new Paganism) is the overall name for modern nature religion. Just as Christianity has many different forms (Catholic, Episcopal, Lutheran, Methodist, and so forth), so does Paganism. Some of the forms of Paganism include Wicca, Witchcraft, Druidism, Shamanism, Odinism, Goddess spirituality, and many others. Although there are differences between the many forms of Paganism, they also have much in common.

✪ Witchcraft and other forms of Paganism have nothing to do with devil worship or Satanism. On the contrary, Paganism teaches the importance of living an upstanding and ethical life, just like any other religion. Wicca, incidentally, is simply an archaic word for Witchcraft, although in practice, Wicca and Witchcraft are slightly different.

✪ Christians subdivide God into a Father, Son, and Holy Spirit. Wiccans do the same thing, only they see God as a Mother and a Father. In other words, as a Mother Goddess and a Father God. In fact, one of the biggest differences between Paganism and Christianity is that Pagans prefer a feminine image of the Goddess over, or in addition to, the traditional masculine image of God. To Pagans, it just seems more natural to see the creator of all things as a Mother. After all, we are all born from a mother!

✪ As you might expect of a nature religion, Pagans love the natural world. To Pagans, it makes no sense to see spirituality as separate from the material world. The Goddess is present in the material world, just as she is present in prayer and meditation. For this reason, Pagans see nature as holy, and many Pagans get involved in recycling and ecological preservation as a way of expressing their religious convictions.

✪ Most Pagans talk about magic—an easily misunderstood term. To Pagans, magic is not about pulling rabbits out of hats, or conjuring up spirits to do one's bidding. Instead, it is best seen as using spiritual power to achieve goals. Most people, not just Pagans, use spiritual power in their daily lives. For example, just about anyone who believes in God will pray for healing when someone is sick. What Christians call prayer, Pagans call magic. It's basically the same thing: relying on spiritual power to achieve our goals and live happier lives. Just as Christians ask for God's blessing through their prayers, Pagans ask for the Goddess' blessing through their magic.

✪ Paganism is basically a new religion. It didn't really exist before the 1940s. But it is based on ancient spirituality (such as the spirituality of the Druids, the ancient priests of Ireland and Scotland), as well as on modern science and psychology. For many Pagans, following this religion is about getting in touch with one's (ancient) roots. For example, the more I have learned about the ancient Celts, the more I admire their civilization and spirituality. Modern Pagans try to honor the old ways of our forefathers and foremothers, who lived close to nature and who believed in Mother Earth as much as in a heavenly Father.

✪ Hundreds of thousands, perhaps even millions, of people around the world follow the Pagan path. Pagans come from all walks of life: rich and poor, male and female, straight and gay, high school dropouts and Ph.D.s. Pagans can be found in every corner of society: as lawyers, teachers, computer program-mers, doctors, nurses, mechanics, and writers. The U.S. Military has a thriving Pagan population, since many Pagan groups consider it an honorable thing to be a warrior. The Military acknowledges Pagans as practicing a valid religion, and many military bases have Pagan chaplains or chaplain assistants.

Now, you may be thinking, "All this is okay, but I still don't like the idea of *Witchcraft*." Let's take a closer look at that.

I grew up in the Lutheran Church, and learned an inter-esting tidbit about Lutheran history. Once upon a time, call-ing somebody a Lutheran was an insult. It meant that the person was a radical, a heretic, a follower of that terrible Martin Luther. But as the Protestant Reformation swept much of Europe, Lutheranism became a noble and honor-able religion. Today, millions of people all over the world are proud to be Lutherans.

Witchcraft is similar. In ancient times, to call somebody a Witch meant to accuse them of using spiritual power to curse or harm others. We now know this was based on super-stition and fear. Meanwhile, scholars have determined that much of what was considered to be "Witchcraft" in ages past may have actually been the nature-based spirituality com-monly practiced in Europe up until the coming of Christian-ity. As people began to see Witchcraft as nature spirituality and not as something harmful, they began to see it as a good and upstanding thing. So today, when someone calls them-selves a Witch, they mean it in a totally positive way.

Some Christians believe that God hates people who aren't good Christians, and God will punish such people in hell. I assume that anyone open-minded enough to read this book does not believe this, but it's still worth mentioning. After all, you may have heard such Christians talk about Paganism (or other non-Christian religions) in a negative way, and even if you don't share their views, they may trouble you. I think it's important to acknowledge that some people think if you don't follow their religion, then you are evil, bad, and basically doomed. People who think this way are called fundamentalists. The tragedy of 9/11 is the logical end-result of the fundamentalist mind. Islamic fundamentalists committed the terrorism of 9/11, but of course the vast majority of Muslims are opposed to terrorism. Sincere followers of Islam think terrorism is horrible and want terrorists to be brought to justice. The dark side of fundamentalism is not limited to Islam. Think of the Christian extremists who have bombed abortion clinics or shot doctors who provided legal abortions. The moral of the story: fundamentalists may think God is on their side, but taken to an extreme, their behavior is hardly Godly.

Only a small number of Christians actually believe that Pagans and other non-Christians are going to go to hell. Incidentally, these Christian fundamentalists not only think Pagans are going to hell, but they think Jews, Buddhists, Hindus, Muslims, and anyone else whose religion is different from their own is doomed. Like most Pagans, I believe these people are intolerant and bigoted. Their viewpoint does not even represent the true spirit of Jesus or the Christian religion, which teaches love, compassion, and forgiveness.

Most Christians believe in a loving God and believe that Jesus taught a message of forgiveness and compassion for others. These values of love, compassion, and forgiveness are for all people, not just Christians. Even though Paganism is not based in the Christian Bible, it is a spiritual path just like Buddhism or Hinduism or any other form of religion. If you are a Christian, you may not agree with all the details of Paganism, but I'm sure you would agree with the main principles of love, healing, and respect for nature. Like many Pagans, I person-ally believe that God (or the Goddess) loves all ethical reli-gions equally: Pagan, Christian, Buddhist, Hindu, and so forth. Many Christians feel the same way. This is the path of toler-ance and respect.

I personally believe that Wiccans and Pagans who try to live good lives are often much closer to the teachings of Jesus than are the fundamentalist Christians who have such ugly opinions about people who are different from themselves.

It is not the purpose of this book to convert you to Pagan-ism, or to dissuade you from participating in your own reli-gion. In fact, among Pagans it is considered impolite to try to get someone to change their religion! Of course, Pagans and Wiccans ask for the same courtesy.

I am very proud to be part of the Pagan community. There are anywhere from 750,000 to 2 million Pagans in the United States alone (it's hard to come up with precise num-bers, because many people practice Paganism on their own, and it's growing so fast that numbers are almost immediately obsolete). It's a sizeable community, but still a minority reli-gion. Nevertheless, research indicates that it is growing rap-idly, meeting the spiritual needs of many more people with each passing year. Today, Pagans are at the forefront of caring for the environment, supporting civil liberties for women and gays and lesbians, and working for religious freedom, not only for Pagans, but also for members of all religions.

I hope you'll see, by reading this book, that Paganism is an honorable, ethical, and spiritual religion. I hope you'll see its goodness and beauty, and how it helps people to live happy, moral, and fulfilling lives. I hope you'll understand it enough to realize that Wiccans and other Pagans have made the right spiritual choice *for themselves*. I don't ask that you agree with every little detail of Paganism, any more than you could agree with every little detail of any other religion. But I do hope you can see the basic beauty of this path.

The rest of this book is arranged in a question and answer format. Feel free to jump around, reading the questions that are of most pressing interest to you. Of course, to get the most well-rounded picture of Wicca and Paganism, read the entire book, and follow up with the books and Websites recommended in questions 79–81.

May the Spirit of Love and Respect guide you always on your life's path.

Part One:

When Someone
You Love
Is Wiccan

Maybe it's your son or daughter, or your next-door neighbor. Maybe it's your best friend, or someone you work with. Whoever it may be, you have just learned that this person walks a spiritual path called by several names, including Wicca, Paganism, and even Witchcraft.

Thank you for making the effort to learn more about this little-known and often-misunderstood spiritual path. Your decision to learn, and not just pass judgment, shows that you are a fair and thoughtful person. It is my hope that this book will give you all the information you need to make an informed, balanced decision about this spiritual path and its role in the life of someone you love.

This book answers more than 80 different questions people commonly ask when trying to learn the basics about nature spirituality. Start with the nine questions here in Part One. These are the fundamentals, covering the most important and pressing issues.

Why would I want to read a book about *Witchcraft?*

This is a book about Paganism, Wicca, and…Witchcraft. Yes, *Witchcraft*. Go ahead, think about all the stereotypes. Ugly old hags riding brooms, and stirring cauldrons in which they're brewing their poisons. Cackling maniacally as they cast their spells designed to hurt people, or as they turn up the heat to cook poor Hansel and Gretel.

Maybe you have a more sophisticated view of Witchcraft. Perhaps you've seen the books about modern Witchcraft for sale at your local metaphysical bookstore. You know that it is a modern religion that began in England in the mid-20th century. It was inspired by scholars who believed that the so-called "Witches" who were burned at the stake in centuries past were actually practicing the old, primal religion of ancient Europe that existed prior to the coming of Christianity. That's much closer to the truth. But in all honesty, it's still not necessarily your first choice of a religion!

This book is an unusual book about Witchcraft. Most of the books about it are written either for college professors who are studying it, or for individuals who are interested in it for themselves. Well, the professorial books are generally expensive and hard to find, so your average bookstore is only going to have the books for people who actually want to be a Witch.

Some of those books are really good, intelligent books filled with thoughtful ideas and interesting perspectives on religion. Others are silly; they pander to the stereotypes of Witches, and promise the reader how to get everything they want out of life just by casting a spell. Real Witches often make fun of those because such books tend to lack spiritual depth.

The book you're holding is written for a different kind of reader. I'm assuming that you are reading this book not because you want to *be* a Witch, but probably because you're either curious, nervous, or fully alarmed because *someone you know* is a Witch. That someone might be a friend, a co-worker, or—gasp! One of your kids. Teenagers are fascinated by the subject of Witchcraft. For some, it's just adolescent rebellion (hey, I bet they're the ones buying all the goofy books on casting spells). But for others, it is a thoughtful, serious interest in a spirituality that's based on nature. Witchcraft is nature spirituality. Witches believe that nature is sacred and holy. Well, in our day, with all the threats to the environment, we need more people to believe nature is sacred, don't you think?

Modern Witchcraft is related to a larger spiritual movement known as Paganism or Neopaganism. Many Witches also use the word Wicca to describe Witchcraft. Later in this book I'll explain the subtle differences between Paganism, Witchcraft, and Wicca, but for now I want to make sure you are familiar with each of these words. For the purposes of this book, I will be using them almost interchangeably. There are some nicknames for Witchcraft, including the craft, the craft of the wise, and the old religion. Just for variety's sake, I'll use those nicknames from time to time. Finally, Wicca can be called nature spirituality or Goddess spirituality, so I'll use those terms as well.

Why would anyone want to call themselves a Witch?

Remember the movie *The Wizard of Oz*, where Glinda asks Dorothy if she's a good Witch or a bad Witch? Dorothy immediately insists she's not a Witch—how could she be, since Witches are old and ugly? Laughing, Glinda points out to Dorothy that she, Glinda, is herself a Witch. Glinda is neither old nor ugly, and Dorothy soon realizes Glinda is indeed a good Witch.

The first lesson Dorothy learns in Oz is that goodness and Witchcraft can coexist. Even though Dorothy has to overcome a particularly nasty bad Witch while in Oz, the distinction has been made: not all Witches are bad, therefore, some Witches can be good. It's important to understand this distinction, for this is the key to understanding why hundreds of thousands of intelligent, mature, spiritually motivated people are today embracing Witchcraft. They are not motivated by Witchcraft's "bad" stereotype, but rather by the goodness that they have found in the craft.

Let's acknowledge the traditional stereotypes. To many people, the words *Witch* and *Witchcraft* conjure up images such as:

- ✪ Ugly old hags stirring cauldrons with noxious fumes spilling out of them.

- ✪ Spiteful sorceresses who cast magic spells meant to hurt people.

- ✪ Some biddy with a wart on her nose who rides a broomstick.

If that's all that Witchcraft is about, why would anyone in their right mind ever want to be a Witch?

These caricatures have more to do with Hollywood than with reality. Real Witches are like most human beings. Some are beautiful, some are plain, most are average. Some are highly evolved individuals with an almost saint-like sense of ethics and compassion, while others are ordinary people who just want their fair share of what life has to offer. In other words, real Witches just don't match up with the Hollywood stereotypes.

Instead of being ugly hags who like to eat children, modern Witches are mostly educated, intelligent, ethical people with an avid interest in the ancient wisdom traditions of Europe and other parts of the world. Modern Witches believe that we can learn to live life in accordance with the inherent wisdom of nature, based on the primal traditions of ancient Europe. And far from eating babies, many Witches are strict vegetarians who insist on consuming only organic produce!

An ethical person dedicated to wisdom certainly sounds better than the Hollywood stereotype of the bad Witch. Still, you may be wondering, why use the words *Witch* and *Witchcraft* at all? Why don't Witches find a less controversial word to describe themselves? The answer is disarmingly simple. Some people like the idea of being a good Witch. They like the aura of mystery, magic, and spiritual power associated with Witchcraft. They study and practice Witchcraft for good reasons, such as learning to be a healer or to become more loving and trusting people. If it's used for good, why not be a Witch?

Some (but not all) modern Witches also use the words *Wiccan* and *Wicca* as alternative names for Witches and Witchcraft, respectively. These words come from the Middle

English word for a male Witch (the female variant is Wicce, but that doesn't get used nearly as much). Others prefer the words *Pagan* and *Paganism*, based on the idea that Witchcraft originated in the Pagan religions of ancient Europe. Over the past 50 years, the words Witchcraft/Witch, Wicca/Wiccan, and Paganism/Pagan have all come to mean slightly different things, distinctions that we'll explore more closely in Part Two. For the purposes of this book, however, these terms are used more or less interchangeably. Which means that there are several words available to describe this spiritual path. If someone likes the words Witch and Witchcraft to describe nature-based religion, they can use them. If they prefer language that's less controversial, they can identify themselves as Pagan or Wiccan.

So Witchcraft isn't about ugly hags riding on brooms?

We looked at how Hollywood plays a role in shaping the stereotypes that persist about Wicca. Believe it or not, what most people think about Witches, Witchcraft, and similar subjects come to us primarily through movies, TV, and popular culture in general.

Who hasn't felt a chill at the cackle of the Wicked Witch of the West as she flew through the air on her broom, painting "Surrender Dorothy" with infernal smoke across the clear blue sky? Who hasn't lumped Witches together with ghosts, monsters, and goblins, thanks to the marketing of kiddie costumes every year at Halloween? If you live in the United

States, you get exposed to plenty of images of Witches, but these images are created by Hollywood and Madison Avenue. They are meant not to teach or enlighten us, but simply to entertain us and make a few bucks.

It's not my purpose here to pick on the entertainment industry, but I do think it's unfortunate how the stereotypes of Witches-as-evil-hags-who-do-nasty-things-with-their-supernatural-powers persist, thanks largely to show business. Part of your job in educating yourself about Witchcraft will be to *un*-learn all the myths from Hollywood about the craft.

Even though some of the images of Witches in popular culture are better than others (most Pagans would take *Harry Potter* over *Rosemary's Baby* any day of the week), none of the pop-culture images of Witchcraft are entirely accurate or fair. Anyone who truly wants to learn about the craft as it is practiced by real people today first must eliminate all the falsehoods that they've seen in print or on the screen over the years.

Here is just a smattering redundant of the misconceptions about Witches that appear in movies or books or elsewhere. If you are knowledgeable about Witchcraft, you'll see how every one of these is erroneous in at least one significant way. If you are not knowledgeable, read this with the understanding that these are inaccurate ideas.

✪ The myth of *Hansel and Gretel*: Witches are ugly hags who eat innocent children.

✪ The myth of *Practical Magic* or *The Craft*: Witches are young, sexy babes, who are morally neutral and given to casting love spells, and need to be careful that they don't get themselves into trouble with their magic.

✪ The myth of the *Harry Potter* series: Witches are only women, because men, after all, are wizards. And while some Witches and wizards are good, others are evil, and use their magic powers to hurt people. You better be careful.

✪ The myth of *Bewitched* or *Sabrina the Teenage Witch*: Witches are good-looking, successful, suburbanite women and girls. But somehow, they seem to always get themselves into some sort of comical mess.

✪ The myth of *Buffy the Vampire Slyer* or *Charmed*: Witches are basically good-hearted people with a certain measure of supernatural ability. But the universe we live in has so much evil nasty stuff in it that the main function of Wicca has to be perpetual vigilance against the forces of darkness.

✪ The myth of *The Witches of Eastwick*: Witches are basically nice women who get duped by the devil.

✪ The myth of *Rosemary's Baby*: Witches are Satan worshipers, not above arranging for the devil to rape an unsuspecting young woman so that she can give birth to his evil son.

✪ The myth of *The Wizard of Oz*: there are good Witches and there are bad Witches. The good Witches fly around in bubbles and look like fairy godmothers. The bad witches are much more striking, with their green skin, flying brooms, ability to appear and disappear in a flash of orange smoke, and their stylish winged-monkey servants. Alas, they easily melt.

✪ The myth of *Bell, Book, and Candle*: Witches can't fall in love, unless they are willing to give up their powers.

✪ The myth of *The Chronicles of Narnia*: Witches are the bad guys.

✪ The myth of *The Blair Witch Project*: Witches are mysterious, unknown figures who live in the dark, unknown woods. They are scary as hell.

✪ The myth of *Monty Python and the Holy Grail*: it's okay to make light of the people who persecuted and killed alleged Witches (although this movie get points for depicting those who persecute Witches as really, really stupid looking).

I'm sure there are others I've left out, but this list will give you a basic sense of just how prominent the image of the Witch is in our culture—and how inaccurate these images are.

Witches don't eat babies or children. They aren't necessarily old, ugly hags, or sexy young women. Wiccans include both women and men, young and old, rich and poor, Ph.Ds and high school dropouts. Most hold down respectable jobs and live in nice homes with their families. Witches, Wiccans, and Pagans don't believe in, let alone worship, Satan or any other devil. Real Witches don't fly on brooms, don't keep winged monkeys as pets, and not one has ever melted when taking a shower. Wiccans fall in love just as much as anyone else, and don't think the universe we live in is a particularly bad place. In fact, most Pagans love the universe as the direct creation of the Goddess they adore.

In short, the average Witch is not that different from the average person, period. Except that they are Witches, instead of being Christian, Jewish, Muslim, or Buddhist.

There's nothing wrong with watching an entertaining film or reading a good book, even if they're not 100 percent accurate in their depiction of Witches (or of anyone else). But it's important to remember that the entertainment business should not be the source of our opinions on Witchcraft or any other topic.

Is Witchcraft evil?

If you learn just one thing from this book, I hope it's this: *Pagans, including Witches and Wiccans, are not Satanists.*

Let me repeat it. The practitioners of modern Paganism, Witchcraft, and Wicca, do not believe in Satan. They do not worship Satan, or talk about him in their rituals. They have nothing to do with devil worship—*period.*

If anything, Pagans are sick and tired of the devil. They just wish he'd go away.

For hundreds of years, Christians have used the words "Witch" and "Witchcraft" to describe devil worshipers and Satanists. That's a Christian idea, and no Wiccans accept it.

Christianity is not perfect. For hundreds of years, Christians believed the sun revolved around the Earth. Up until recent times, many Christians believed slavery was okay and most Christians believed wives should obey their husbands for no other reason than their gender. Today, nearly all people, including most Christians, realize that these erroneous beliefs were mistakes made by their religion in the past.

Well, the Christian idea about Witchcraft was also a mistake.

Most scholars believe that once Christianity became the dominant religion in Europe, it adopted a policy of intolerance toward the older religions that existed in Europe before it. These older religions were regarded as superstition, sorcery, and eventually as devil worship. But the devil is a *Christian* concept, not a native European idea. Since the Christians believed in the devil, they assumed that anyone practicing a religion other than Christianity must be a devil-worshiper. In other word, they projected their concept of Satan onto non-Christians. And then they called the non-Christians heretics…and Witches.

By the 15th century, intellectuals in the Christian church were writing books about how to hunt down these alleged devil-worshipers. This led to one of the most shameful chapters of human history, the 250-year period in which tens of thousands of people (mostly women) were killed for the "crime" of Witchcraft.

Today, most historians believe that the so-called Witches who were killed throughout Europe and in U. S. towns such as Salem, Massachusetts, were not really Witches at all, at least not how we understand the term today. In fact, most of those people would probably have thought of themselves as Christians. Some of them may have been herbalists or midwives, using ancient natural wisdom as healers. But none of them, so far as we can tell, were ever involved in an organized religion of devil worship. That, apparently, was just the paranoid fantasy of the men who took it upon themselves to rid the world of evil.

In our day, we still have people who make unilateral decisions that there are groups of people who are "evil" and must therefore be destroyed. Adolf Hitler built a political career around his belief that Jews needed to be exterminated. In more recent years, terrorists such as Osama Bin Laden have been driven by hatred of Americans, seeing the United States as "the great Devil" that must be eradicated.

Again and again, these people who attack the evil they see in others are doing what psychologists call *projection*. In other words, instead of taking responsibility for their own problems and working to make their own lives better, these disturbed people blame others for their misfortunes, decide that those whom they blame are evil, and then try to destroy them. They think they are the righteous warriors on a mission from God. But to everyone else, they appear to be merely deranged, deluded, and (unfortunately) dangerous.

Many feminists believe that the attack on so-called Witches in the 15th through 17th centuries was really an attack on women. Scholars estimate that as many as 95 percent of those killed for Witchcraft were women. Why would a culture be so convinced that women outnumber men in their capacity for "evil" on a ratio of 19 to 1?

From the vantage point of the 20th century, we know that for thousands of years, women have endured second-class status in many parts of the world. In Christianity, God is a male, and (except in recent years) his priests were all males. Many Christian theologians interpreted the story of Eve and the Serpent in the Bible and concluded that it was woman's fault that human beings were "fallen." Perhaps the Witch craze represents a hysterical period in a culture that was so sexist that it actually turned on its own women, killing them instead of loving and cherishing them.

Many Pagans believe that the second-class status of women throughout much of history is linked to the idea that God is only a male. For Witches, seeing Spirit as both Goddess and God is acknowledging a simple fact of nature: human beings, along with most other life forms, reproduce through sexual means, requiring both a male and a female to create new life. Both are necessary to create new life. The idea that a male God, by himself, could create all things simply goes against nature. And in a society where only the male God is worshiped, what is to be done with females? Well, since the beginning of Christianity, the male God had an adversary: the devil. If human males are more like God, wouldn't that imply that human females are more naturally like the devil? It's no wonder so many women were put to death for the "crime" of devil worship.

The way most Wiccans see it, the universe is not dominated by a good God and an evil devil, but is the loving creation of a feminine Goddess and her masculine God. When Christians believe in a God and a devil, that suggests the universe is a giant, cosmic battlefield. But the way Wiccans see it, the universe is a sensuous marriage chamber, where Goddess and God embrace each other in love. This is a way of seeing the universe that honors women and men equally.

Witches and Wiccans do not believe in a devil. Pagans cannot worship the devil, since they don't believe in him to begin with. Indeed, Wiccans actually feel sorry for people who believe in the devil, since their vision of the universe is much more terrifying and frightening than the Pagan view.

Some fundamentalist Christians insist that Witches are under the domination of the devil—and when writers like me say that's not true, they say this just means we've been deceived. Alas, this is a no-win situation. The more Witches provide thoughtful, balanced, intelligent reasons as to why the devil has nothing to do with Wicca, the more the fundamentalists will just chant their refrain: "You've been deceived." This means that the fundamentalists really don't want to listen to our perspective. They've made up their minds that they are right and we are wrong. This is worrisome. There are fundamentalist groups active in the United States today that insist that Witchcraft, homosexuality, and other "sins" should be made into capital crimes for which the death penalty ought to be meted out. With those kinds of ideas going around, I have to wonder who is really the voice of evil: the nature-loving Witches, or the fundamentalist extremists who say Witches ought to be executed?

All that Pagans and Wiccans ask of non-Pagans is that you understand Witchcraft on its own terms. Wicca and Witchcraft have nothing to do with the devil or Satan. Period.

What *is* Witchcraft?

The last couple of questions have looked at what Witchcraft is not. It's not about ugly old hags riding brooms and eating babies; nor is it a religion of devil-worship.

So what *is* it?

Here's a brief overview of the main qualities of Witchcraft and Wicca. Most of these points will be expanded in greater detail.

> ✪ Wicca is a spiritual path. In other words, it is a way for people to find meaning and purpose in their life through spirituality.

✪ Witches believe in God, but see God as having two dimensions: a masculine and a feminine dimension. Witches call the female dimension the Goddess, and the male dimension the God.

✪ Witches don't regard nature as just a creation of the God and the Goddess, like a painting is a creation of an artist. This implies that there is some sort of separation between the creator and the creation. Rather, Witches would be more likely to see the natural world as the "body" of the Goddess and the God, just like the human body is the physical dimension of the human soul. This is why Wiccans consider it important to revere nature. When one reveres nature, one is revering the Goddess and the God as well.

✪ Witchcraft is a system of healing. Historically, the Witches were the wise women and men who understood how to use herbs and other natural tools to help heal the sick. Many of today's Witches see their craft as a tool to help bring about spiritual healing to individuals as well as to planet Earth as a whole.

✪ Not all Witches would call Witchcraft a religion, mainly because they're uncomfortable with the abuses found in other religions (may there never be a Wiccan priestess on TV raising millions of dollars for her selfish purposes!). But strictly speaking, Wicca is indeed a religion: a system of meaning and purpose that involves reverence for the God and the Goddess, a moral code, and a set of spiritual practices.

✪ The moral code of Witchcraft is called the *Wiccan Rede*. Many versions of the Rede exist, but they include this essential statement: If you harm none, do what you will. In other words, Wiccan ethics balance personal freedom (do what you will) with a commitment to respect the rights and freedom of others (harm none).

✪ Witches see the God and the Goddess as two aspects of a unified Spirit. But they also see ancient mythology as a helpful tool for learning about the Goddess and the God. Thus, Witches enjoy learning about the mythic Gods and Goddesses from cultures all around the world. Some of the most loved include ancient Greek, Roman, Egyptian, Norse, and Celtic myths.

✪ Witches believe in magic. The simplest way to define magic is spiritual power or energy. In other words, Witches believe such a spiritual power exists, and that it is morally acceptable to use such power for good purposes. So much of the activity that Witches engage in relates to learning about, and how to use, the energy of magic.

✪ Wiccans perform religious ceremonies called rituals. These usually take place in the evening, most often on the night of the full moon or the new moon, or on the solstices, equinoxes, or four other days considered particularly holy (including Halloween, the night most commonly associated with Witchcraft). The purpose of these rituals is to honor the Goddess and the God, and to generate magical energy, usually for the purpose of healing. Whereas

Christians and members of other religions typically pray for healing when someone is sick, Witches work magic as a way of asking the Goddess to heal the sick.

✪ Witches generally adopt a "live and let live" attitude toward other religions. They accept religious diversity as a normal fact of life. They feel the only problem with other religions is when they encourage their members to be intolerant of those whose beliefs are different from their own.

✪ Wiccans are optimistic about life. They believe the world we live in as basically good, and that the God and the Goddess are loving deities.

✪ Finally, most Witches believe in life after death; the most common idea is that after death the soul goes to a paradise known as the Summerland; eventually the soul can reincarnate in a new body.

To summarize: Witchcraft is a positive, life-affirming religious and spiritual practice. It is based on loving the Goddess and the God, performing rituals designed to honor the Goddess and the God, and seeking magic (spiritual power) to be used for good purposes, such as helping to heal the sick. Witches have a liberal, but strong, ethical code, based on the idea that personal freedom is okay but harming others is not.

What's so good about Witchcraft?

Why do Witches believe it's a good thing to be a Witch?

As I mentioned in the last chapter, Witches have a positive outlook on life. To Witches, the world is not some vale of tears that a person must suffer through before receiving a pie in the sky, by and by. On the contrary, Witches believe that life here on Earth is already a miracle. And even though there's pain and suffering here on Earth, that is not evidence that life is bad, but simply a challenge to put the energies of magic into practice. Witches believe magic is an energy for creating more love, trust, and healing in the world. If enough people believed in magic, perhaps there wouldn't be suffering at all!

The word "good" basically means that something is "of God." As for what is good about Witchcraft, well, because it is a spiritual practice designed to help its followers get closer to God (and the Goddess), that is naturally what makes it good.

Witches believe in healing. Even scientists are beginning to acknowledge that spirituality and prayer play an important role in helping sick people to get better. Witches find that their prayers (magic) and rituals make a real difference in helping their loved ones to get over diseases and traumas.

Witches believe in personal responsibility. No Witch can ever say "the devil made me do it" because Witches don't believe in a devil. Instead of blaming some bad guy with a pitchfork, Witches teach that each person must take responsibility for his or her own actions.

Witchcraft teaches respect for the environment. The world we live in today is a world where pollution, toxic waste, runaway population growth, and many other calamities are threatening our beleaguered planet. Most religions have very little to say about taking care of Mother Nature. Witches, however, believe Mother Nature is an aspect of the Goddess, so Witches teach that recycling, conservation, and other environmental practices are an important part of spirituality. In Witchcraft, worshipping the Goddess and taking care of the environment go hand in hand.

Witchcraft teaches respect for women. Any religion that worships a Great Goddess will also be a religion where women receive honor and respect. In many Wiccan groups, leadership starts with a woman known as the High Priestess. Wicca teaches that men and women are equal and should share power and authority equally, not only in religious matters, but in all aspects of life. There are no second-class citizens in the craft.

Witches do not believe in scare tactics. Some religions use concepts such as judgment and hell as a way to frighten people into never questioning religious authorities. This is a misguided practice, for it can lead to people feeling guilt-ridden over normal human thoughts and actions. Witches believe that God is kind and loving, and would not condone using fear as a tool for motivating people to believe. Wicca's motto is "Perfect Love and Perfect Trust"—not "repent or burn!"

Because few Wiccan groups own real estate or pay their ministers, Witchcraft rarely requires pledging or other financial commitments. There are a few large covens, usually in major cities, that do ask members to make a pledge, but these are the exception rather than the rule. Most Wiccan groups cost nothing more than the time to volunteer. "Love offerings" may be taken to defray the cost of snacks and other expenses but that's the extent to which donations are solicited. You don't make a huge financial commitment, so you never have to worry about your money being misused.

Witches respect the individual. The Wiccan Rede is a statement of personal freedom: if it harms none, do what you will. Witches don't believe in trying to convert others or in guilt-tripping people who decide Wicca isn't for them and leave the religion. In other words, it is the opposite of a religious "cult."

These are just a few examples of how Witchcraft functions as an ethical, moral, positive force in the lives of its adherents. Ask any Witch if being involved in the craft has helped them to be a better person, and they'll almost always say "Yes!" What more could you ask of a religion, than to help people to live better, happier, more ethical and fulfilling lives?

Do Witches worship God?

Most Witches prefer to use a gender-free word such as "Spirit," but strictly speaking, yes, they worship God.

However, it must be said that the Wiccan concept of God is different from that of most Jews, Christians, or Muslims.

The religions that originated in the Middle East almost universally depict God as a supreme male entity. He is a He-God. In recent years, some feminists and other liberal thinkers have tried to show how "God" really exists beyond the distinctions of male or female gender. That's a nice theory, but when it comes to how people practice their religion, virtually all

Jews, Christians, and Muslims still worship the Big Daddy in the Sky. To Witches, Big Daddy is only half of God. The other half is the Goddess, the Big Momma.

Witches prefer to say "Spirit" when referring to the One Ultimate Source of Life. Spirit truly transcends the limitations of gender and sexuality.

To help differentiate Witchcraft's ideas of God from those of other religions, Witches generally use "the" in front of the words God and Goddess. Witches will refer to the feminine face of Spirit as *the* Goddess, while the masculine face of Spirit is *the* God.

The Goddess and the God are united together in the one ultimate Spirit. This Spirit, in Wiccan terms, is the approximate equivalent of the ultimate God as worshipped by other religions.

So, while the words and symbols are different from those used by other religions, the spiritual heart of their religious devotion is the same.

Is Witchcraft safe?

Concepts such as magic may be unfamiliar to you, and therefore you may be wondering if Witchcraft is safe. You may be worried that it's like using drugs, and can lead to insanity or mental instability. Or perhaps it can lead to spiritual problems.

Indeed, some people who write about magic insist that it is a potentially dangerous power, and should never be used except under the supervision of an established expert. Those kinds of ideas can be unsettling, especially to parents whose children are interested in the old religion.

Naturally, an element of risk exists in all human endeavor. You cannot get in a car or board an airplane without assuming some degree of risk. But Witchcraft is certainly not risky in that sense. Because Witches believe it is wrong to harm others, going to a Wiccan ritual is entirely safe on a physical level. Any risk that would come out of attending a Witch ritual would be something not directly related to Wicca. For example, if the ritual were held in an unsafe neighborhood, there would be a risk of getting mugged. But that same risk would be there if you attended a Christian event in the same area.

Could Witchcraft be dangerous and harmful on a psychological level? No more so than any other religion. Probably the biggest risk associated with Witchcraft is that someone would become so caught up in the world of rituals and mythology that they neglect other aspects of their life. But that kind of behavior could just as easily happen to someone who becomes a Christian zealot or who gets obsessed about any other pursuit.

Spiritually, Wicca is one of the safest of religions, since it promotes personal responsibility and intellectual liberty. Unlike a cult, Wicca and other forms of Paganism do not require a person to believe or behave in a certain way.

Any dangers that could possibly be associated with Witchcraft are just the normal risks of being alive. Indeed, most Witches would argue that their religion is highly safe, promoting positive values such as love, trust, and healing. It bases its ethics on taking personal responsibility for one's own happiness and well-being. These kinds of values are consistent with what many psychologists would say are necessary for good

mental health. If Witchcraft helps you to become more loving, more trusting, and more self-reliant, then it is not only a
safe activity, but actually one that promotes mental health and
personal wellness.

Why should we take Witchcraft seriously? Isn't it just a big joke?

In answering question 1, I mentioned the silly books on spellcasting that you can find in just about any bookstore. They
have goofy titles, such as *How to Turn Your Ex-Boyfriend into
a Toad & Other Spells For Love, Wealth, Beauty and Revenge*.
Books like these tend to sell quite well, although I suspect
they sell more for their humor than their spirituality. Still, it
leaves you wondering: can Witchcraft really be serious? Isn't
it just a put-on, or some lame idea for teenagers who have no
self-confidence?

Well, I can't be responsible for what the publishing world
thinks will sell. And certainly there is a market for books
about casting spells and turning guys into amphibians. But
to limit Pagan spirituality to that level would be like saying
Christianity is nothing more than a tool for making the old
man with the gray beard up in heaven accept you. Just as there
are childish ways to think about any religion, Witchcraft can
be reduced to the childish level of casting-a-spell-to-get-what-
you-want. Unfortunately, many books are published on precisely that level, and they give the craft a bad name.

But for many people, Paganism is about living an upstanding, responsible life in harmony with our natural environment. Concepts like magic and spells are spiritual tools for healing, similar to how Christians use prayer. Many Pagans are dedicated scholars who study ancient mythology, archaeology, and culture to try to find wisdom that can be applied to modern life. For all of these people, this is a very serious spiritual path indeed.

Paganism is serious enough to be one of the fastest growing religions on Earth today. For a number of reasons, an exact figure of how many people practice Paganism is difficult to attain. But recent studies have estimated anywhere from 750,000 to 2 million people in North America alone practice some form of Paganism, and those numbers are growing. This means there are more Pagans in North America than there are Unitarians or Quakers.

If you find yourself thinking that Paganism is silly, that's really just a variation of the more common prejudice that Paganism is evil. Whether seen as evil or silly, these ideas are based on misconceptions, and they serve to dismiss the genuine and heartfelt spiritual experience of thousands of people. For the interest of fairness and respect for others' religious choices, refrain from dismissing nature spirituality as a joke. Take the time to learn about it with the same degree of respect and careful attention you would pay to any unfamiliar subject.

Part Two:

Understanding
Witchcraft

You know that Witchcraft is not the same thing as devil worship and doesn't involve human sacrifice. But there's still a lot that you don't know. What's the difference between a Witch and a Wiccan? Why don't male Witches use the word warlock? Why is there so much secrecy surrounding this stuff?

The questions explored in this section will deepen your basic understanding of nature spirituality. This builds on the material presented in Part One, and is intended to help you feel more comfortable with the ins and outs of the Pagan world. Although there's much about Paganism that may seem odd or unusual to outsiders, the more you learn about it, the more sensible it becomes.

What is the difference between Witchcraft and Wicca?

Up to now, I've been using the words *Witchcraft* and *Wicca* pretty much interchangeably. The only real difference I've mentioned is that some people prefer the word Wicca because it doesn't have the connotations and stereotypes associated with Witchcraft.

In terms of language, they mean the same thing. But in terms of contemporary usage, there are subtle differences between them.

Wicca is a middle English word for "male Witch." The female version is Wicce. For reasons no one really knows, the modern craft community has embraced Wicca as a generic word for Witchcraft, and invented the word Wiccan to refer to both males and females.

As I mentioned in Part One, many people are drawn to Witchcraft because of the mystery and romance they believe is associated with the old religion. These people like the idea of being a Witch, even if this means that non-Witches sometimes misunderstand them. Many people who identify as Witches believe that the craft goes back hundreds, if not thousands of years. After all, Witches are talked about in the Bible, in the writings of Shakespeare, and in the folklore of fairy tales from around the world. To be a Witch, therefore, is to participate in an ancient tradition of magic and folk healing.

Wicca, even though it is a medieval word, is used in our time to describe a distinctly modern religious practice, stemming from the mid-20th century or so, that is based on or inspired by traditions of magic, folk healing, and Goddess worship that have historically been associated with Witchcraft.

Thus, people who prefer to identify themselves as Witches tend to stress the ancient roots of the craft as a traditional healing practice, while people who prefer to identify themselves as Wiccan tend to stress the modern face of the craft as a new religious movement.

Some Wiccans insist that the contemporary craft is strictly a modern phenomenon, that was *inspired* by Witchcraft of old, but not directly related to it. In response to this, some of the people who identify themselves as Witches have taken the position that *real* Witchcraft is ancient, while Wicca is merely a modern pseudo-Witchcraft.

Meanwhile, there are plenty of others (including myself) who feel that arguing over the real (or perceived) differences between Witchcraft and Wicca is a waste of time. In a way, the quibbling over the meaning of words like Witch and Wiccan seems about as absurd as the fighting between Catholics and Protestants. And yet it goes on and on.

But just as both Catholics and Protestants are Christian, so it is that both Witches and Wiccans are practitioners of modern Paganism (of course, to muddy the waters even further, not all Wiccans or Witches like to be called Pagans). Witches and Wiccans have far more in common than not. In truth, many use the two terms interchangeably. However, it's important to be aware that some people in the Pagan community like to be called one but not the other, or believe there are real differences between what the two words mean.

What is the difference between Witchcraft, Wicca, and other forms of Paganism?

The difference between Wicca and Witchcraft exists mostly in the minds of certain people in the Pagan community. Some people see it as the difference between an ancient healing practice and a modern religious revival, but even this is more a difference of degree than of kind. But there really is a difference between Paganism and Wicca/Witchcraft.

Wicca and Witchcraft are forms of Paganism. Every Witch or Wiccan is a Pagan, but every Pagan is not necessarily a Witch or Wiccan. In its modern usage, Paganism refers to religions or spiritual systems based on the religious or spiritual practices of ancient, pre-Christian Europe or northern Africa. Actually, Wicca and Witchcraft are not entirely based on pre-Christian spirituality. But they are partially based on it, which makes them Pagan.

There are other spiritual movements happening in the world today that are also Pagan, but are emphatically not Wiccan or Witchcraft. These include:

- ✪ Druidism, based on reviving the ancient priesthood of the Celtic nations.

- ✪ Asatru or Odinism, based on a similar revival of Norse and Teutonic religion.

- ✪ Similar movements dedicated to reviving Egyptian, Greek, Roman, or Baltic spirituality.

Paganism describes a wide variety of new religious movements. In fact, there are increasing numbers of groups that combine from a variety of sources (including Wicca) that define themselves as "eclectic Pagan." Others, such as Druidism or Asatru, are based on strict research into the heritage of a specific culture, and therefore are not like Wicca, which tends to be rather multi-cultural in its outlook.

If you ever meet someone whose spirituality is based on Druidism or Asatru, you would be correct to call him a Pagan; but you would be wrong if you called him a Wiccan or a Witch.

Is there more than one kind of Witchcraft?

Just as Christianity can be subdivided into a plethora of different churches (Catholic, Orthodox, Episcopal, Methodist, Baptist, Lutheran, Presbyterian, etc.), the same holds true with the world of Witchcraft. Many different traditions or lineages of Wicca and Witchcraft exist. This is important to understand because the lineages often have subtle but real differences in terms of philosophy, practice, or even social/political orientation.

The man largely credited with launching the modern Witchcraft movement was Gerald B. Gardner, a retired British Civil Servant who wrote several books about his involvement with a Witch coven in the 1950s. Gardner became world famous, and until his death in 1962, initiated a number of people into his version of Witchcraft. His students and followers became known as Gardnerian Witches.

In the years that followed, however, other people appeared on the Wiccan scene, some of whom were students of Gardner's who broke away from his tradition. Others claimed they had received instruction in Witchcraft from sources independent of Gardner. Over time, several distinct versions of Wicca emerged, in addition to the Gardnerian lineage:

- ✪ Alexandrian Witchcraft was named after its founder, Alex Sanders.

- ✪ Seax (Saxon) and Picti (Scottish) Witchcraft were founded by a former student of Gardner's, Raymond Buckland.

- ✪ Dianic (feminist) Witchcraft was made popular by the writings of a California feminist and Witch, Z. Budapest.

- ✪ Faery (fairy) Wicca was taught by a man named Victor Anderson; one of his students, Starhawk, founded the Reclaiming tradition; another, Francesca De Grandis, founded the Third Road tradition.

- ✪ Various traditions exist, including Traditional (Cochranian) Witchcraft, the Unicorn Tradition, the New Reformed Orthodox Order of the Golden Dawn, the Georgian Tradition, the Minoan Sisterhood, the Blue Star tradition, and on and on the list goes.

Since the mid-1970s, many people have been inspired to create new Wiccan groups, claiming no lineage or tradition from teachers, other than reading a book or two on the subject. Although traditionalist Witches sometimes accuse these "book Witches" of being unauthentic and not knowing what they're doing, increasing numbers of people are reading books on Wicca and performing the rituals and ceremonies from the information found in the books, without worrying about finding a teacher or joining an existing lineage.

One of the characteristics of Witchcraft is that it has no central authority. There is no pope or bishop of Witchcraft. Aside from a few Witches who become well-known to the Wiccan community at large (such as Gardner or Starhawk), no one could ever claim the right to speak for all Wiccans. In other words, if you meet up with a group of Witches in your town, they will in all likelihood have no one to answer to, except possibly a mentor to whom their leadership turns for guidance. This is a mixed blessing. Each group of Witches is autonomous; that is to say, it governs itself. But without the resources of a centralized authority, many Wiccan groups fail, or at the very least devote lots of energy to solving the same problems over and over again. However, most Witches would say that the freedom and autonomy that comes from having no centralized authority more than makes up for the lack of resources.

Some Wiccan groups have come together to form networks that operate on a regional or national level. These groups can often assist in providing legal, financial, or other assistance to the member groups, while respecting the autonomy of the local group. One example of this kind of network is the Covenant of the Goddess, an organization of various Wiccan groups and individuals throughout the United States.

What are the differences between the kinds of Witchcraft? In many cases, the distinctions are minimal, aside from tracing the group's lineage back to a different founder. However, some groups (especially those with origins in Great

Britain) tend to be very formal and structured, while other groups (especially those with a feminist orientation) or much more loosely organized and often governed by consensus. This broad distinction may be thought of as "traditional" or "feminist" versions of Wicca. The traditionalists often are more politically conservative or libertarian, while the feminists tend toward a more liberal stance. The traditionalists tend to emphasize ritual and magic, while the feminists emphasize community and social activism. Once upon a time, traditionalist Witches and feminist Witches often were sharply critical of one another, but over time, the distinctions between the two groups have softened.

Is Witchcraft hereditary?

Especially in the early years of the modern Witchcraft movement, many of the people who published books on the craft said that they were taught Witchcraft by a family member, such as a grandmother. Alex Sanders and Sybil Leek were two famous Witches who fell into this category.

Many other Witches, however, have made no such claim. From Gerald Gardner to Starhawk to Phyllis Curott (a Wiccan High Priestess who is also a successful Manhattan lawyer), many people come to Witchcraft simply by answering an inner call, an intuitive sense that this is the right spiritual path for them.

Some Witches and Wiccans place a great emphasis on family lineage, believing that magical or psychic powers are a genetically inherited talent, just like musical or artistic ability. Others scoff at the whole idea of hereditary Witchcraft. It seems that the grandmothers who supposedly taught the ancient secrets were always dead before their grandchildren went public with their teachings. One prominent Witch even said to me that she calls this the "Dead Granny Syndrome"— the idea that someone can claim to be a Wiccan leader just because their granny (now dead) trained them in the ways of the craft. Since Granny isn't around to contradict this claim, who's to challenge it?

When authors such as Sanders and Leek were publishing their books, Wicca was still a relatively young phenomenon. Most people who were attracted to the craft wanted to study an ancient tradition. There's no evidence that ancient Witchcraft exists (if it ever did), but if someone claimed that they learned an authentic tradition from their granny, well, that might sound good to a prospective student. Nowadays, however, many students seem happy enough to learn from any teacher with knowledge to share, whether that teacher gained the knowledge from another teacher, a book, or even a dead Granny.

In the end it doesn't really matter if Witchcraft (or magical power) is hereditary or not. Some people think it's important. But others could care less. As the people who became Witches a generation ago mature and have families, they have the same experience raising children that members of other religions have. Some of their children embrace Wicca, while others rebel against it. The children of Wiccan families are no different than anyone else.

Why are male Witches not called wizards or warlocks?

One of the biggest ways in which modern Witchcraft differs from the stereotypes of Hollywood is in the language for male Witches. Both men and women are called Witches or Wiccans. The words *wizard* and *warlock* are simply not used. Just as both men and women within Christianity are called Christians, and both men and women within Judaism are called Jews, both men and women within Witchcraft are called Witches. There is no distinction based on gender.

Warlock comes from an ancient word that means *oath breaker*. For this reason, some Witches teach that this word refers to a Witch who was expelled from a coven, presumably for misconduct of some sort. Thus, to call a Witch a warlock would be an insult.

The distinction between Witches and wizards is more subtle. In centuries past, there were two kinds of magic: high magic and low magic. High magic was very academic, often practiced by educated men (sometimes even by Christian priests). Low magic involved the wisdom of common people, who would use herbs and other natural ingredients to help heal the sick. A wizard would be a practitioner of the high school of magic, while a Witch would be a practitioner of folk magic. Since modern Witchcraft draws so much inspiration from folk healing traditions, it makes sense that all practitioners, whether male or female, be called Witches.

What is the pentacle, and why do Witches wear it?

One of the most common symbols of Wicca and Witchcraft is the pentacle—the five pointed star surrounded by a circle. This symbol appears on the cover of many books on Wicca and Witchcraft. It also is a common symbol worn as a pendant or an insignia in a ring. Just as Christians wear a cross or Jews wear a Star of David, many Witches choose to wear a pentacle. It is the single most common symbol of the old religion. The star, by itself, is called a pentagram. When it is enclosed in a circle, it is a pentacle.

There is nothing evil or dangerous about the pentacle. It is a symbol with spiritual meaning that Witches find beautiful and comforting.

According to the teachings of many traditions in Witchcraft, the universe is made up of five elements: fire, air, water, earth, and spirit. All things are somehow related to one or more of these elements. Take the human body for example: our lungs represent the element air; our blood stream symbolizes water. Our flesh and bones are linked to earth, while the mind is related to fire. The soul, of course, is related to the element spirit.

Mother Earth has a similar link to the elements. The atmosphere is air, while the oceans and other bodies of water represent water. The soil and rocks symbolize earth, while the molten core of the planet is the source of her fire. Spirit is related to the Goddess herself—the consciousness of Mother Earth whom Witches revere.

The pentagram is a symbol of the elements. The top point of the star is the element spirit. Going clockwise around the star, the other four points represent water, fire, earth, and air. Because the top point of the pentagram represents spirit, it symbolizes the importance that spirit has over the other four elements. Thus, a pentagram (and a pentacle) both stand for spirituality governing matter.

The circle that surrounds the pentagram in a pentacle stands for eternity. Thus, the star represents the material world, while the circle represents the eternal cycle of time. Together, the two symbols of the pentagram represent the totality of the universe, encompassing both space and time. Because Witches see the universe as sacred (as the manifestation of the Goddess and the God), wearing a symbol of the universe is itself a reverent and spiritual thing to do.

What is a magical name? Why do Witches use it?

If you have looked at some of the books available that have been written by Wiccans, you will notice that many of them have colorful names, such as Lady Sabrina, Starhawk, Silver Ravenwolf, Amber K, and Ashleen O'Gaea. If you attend a gathering of Witches, you'll find that many of them use chosen names that differ from their legal names. In fact, in some Wiccan groups, it is a requirement that a person adopt a chosen name for use within Wiccan contexts. This is known as the magical name or religious name.

Of course, not all Wiccan authors use magical names. Gerald Gardner, Phyllis Curott, Raymond Buckland, Gerina

Dunwich, and Patricia Telesco all publish books under their legal names. In some Wiccan circles, a person does not need to use a magical name (unless he or she wants to). This points out an important thing to remember when learning about Witchcraft: it is a diverse community and there are exceptions to every rule. Incidentally, many of the Wiccan authors who publish under their legal name, still have or had a magical name that they use among other Wiccans. Gardner, for example, went by the magical name Scire.

Choosing a magical name is similar to how Roman Catholic children choose a confirmation name. It symbolizes taking on a new personality or a new aspect of the personality. When a person begins to study Witchcraft seriously, he or she expects to grow spiritually. The magical name is a symbol of this new growth.

The folklore behind magical names is that during the times of the persecution of Witches, people who practiced the old religion needed to keep their religion secret from the authorities. Thus, they would get in the habit of using nicknames as a way to maintain secrecy and privacy. It was customary during the Witch craze for the authorities to torture their suspects, in order to get them to reveal who else in the community was practicing Witchcraft. If one Witch were arrested and tortured, he or she would only be able to tell the magical or nicknames of the other Witches, thus protecting them from being apprehended.

It's a charming story, but doesn't have much historical value. As we have already seen, most of the people arrested for "Witchcraft" in centuries past did not practice anything resembling modern Wicca. Furthermore, in the small villages where most Witches would have lived, everyone would have known everyone else, so what good would magical names be in protecting against torture? Under torture, a person would tell all that he or she knew—magical names, real names, whatever.

Even if there is no historical reason for adopting a magical name, it still can be a meaningful spiritual event, just as first communion is a meaningful event in the lives of Christians. It is a rite of passage, a step on the path toward becoming a Witch.

Witches find inspiration for their magical names in many sources. Many take the names of Gods or Goddesses from mythology. Others prefer names based in nature, such as the name of a tree or animal. Others might take a name that is entirely new; I know one person who took a beautiful name, Numina, which is based on the word numinous, meaning "spiritual presence."

Once a person takes a magical name, it is considered impolite to refer to that person by their legal name when in private settings with other Witches. It is also impolite to use their magical name when in public settings or in mixed company.

Why is there so much secrecy surrounding Witchcraft?

Part of the mysterious nature of modern Witchcraft is the aura of secrecy surrounding it. Like the Masons, many Witch covens function essentially as a secret society. When a person is initiated (joins) into a Wiccan coven, they often must take an oath of secrecy. Of course, the Masons and other secret societies do the same thing. But Witches tend to be even more secretive, since they don't have lodges and often have no way for outsiders to get in touch with them. It is rare to find a Wiccan coven listed in the phone book. Most Witches can be found only through word of mouth, although more and more groups do have Websites, or are listed in special directories published within the Pagan/Wiccan community. Still, a person needs to know where to look to find a group or groups in his or her local area.

Why the secrecy? What is there to hide?

As with magical names, there is a romanticized reason for the secrecy, and a more historically accurate, practical reason. First, the romanticized reason. According to Wiccan lore, Goddess and nature worshipers were not always so secretive about their spirituality. But when the persecution of Witches began in earnest during the late middle ages, the Witches were forced to go underground. Witchcraft became a secret society. Even though Witches enjoy civil freedoms today that were denied them for many years, most remain secretive out of respect for the longstanding tradition of hiddenness.

This reason for secrecy has more to do with myth than history. Because there is no evidence of organized Witchcraft before the 20th century, there's no reason to believe Witch groups ever needed to function under such a cloak of secrecy (of course, some Witches will tell you there's no evidence of Witchcraft precisely because they were so successful at staying hidden). But regardless of the historical accuracy behind the secrecy myth, modern Witchcraft finds secrecy useful for a practical reason: unfortunately, discrimination and prejudice against people who practice Witchcraft is very real in our society. Yes, even in the early 21st century, people lose their jobs, their leases, and even custody of their children because they practice Witchcraft. Sometimes non-Witches are too quick to assume that Witchcraft is something evil and bad, and then act in unfair prejudicial ways toward Witches. This is religious discrimination, and it's wrong. But it happens. So, for many Witches, being discreet about their spirituality has been a way to avoid facing discrimination.

However, more and more Witches refuse to stay hidden just because they fear discrimination. Especially among younger people, there is an increasing feeling that Witches deserve their religious freedom as much as anyone else. So perhaps in the future, Wiccan groups will be more publicly visible.

What's the big deal about the "burning times"?

One of the most important keys to understanding modern Witchcraft and Wicca is the tragic period in history known as the "burning times." Beginning approximately in the mid-15th century and extending all the way into the early 18th century (a period of more than 250 years), civil and religious authorities in Europe and parts of North America engaged in an intensive process of hunting for, convicting, and executing alleged Witches. Conservative estimates are that some 40,000 people, nearly all of whom were women, were killed for this supposed crime. Other scholars have estimated anywhere from 100,000 to 250,000 people may have been killed during the burning times. To destroy thousands of lives for religious reasons is an unspeakable horror, and one that our society has never fully addressed. The fact that most of these alleged Witches were women suggests that our society went through a horrible dark time when we, as a people, literally turned on our own wives, mothers, and daughters.

About a hundred years ago, the fashionable theory was that the alleged Witches killed during the burning times were actually practitioners of a surviving Pagan religion. Today, that theory has fallen out of favor, and most historians simply see the burning times as a terrible period of mass delusion and hysteria. Still, the Pagan theory of the burning times was part of what inspired Gerald Gardner and others of his generation to create a new version of Witchcraft for the modern age.

Today's Witches regard the burning times with the same kind of mythic reverence that Jews feel toward the Exodus from Egypt or that Christians feel toward the death and resurrection of Jesus. In other words, this historical event plays a large role in shaping the modern Witch's identity. Wiccans today feel that their religion is a gentle, peaceful, nature-based spirituality; they also feel that the culture we live in has historically been unfair to nature religions. From the Roman soldiers who massacred the Druids in Great Britain, to the Christians who burned the alleged Witches, all the way up to the hostility that European immigrants showed toward Native American religions in the 19th and 20th centuries, it seems that we live in a world where nature religion is attacked and its practitioners are persecuted. For this reason, modern Witches believe they need to be discreet about their spirituality, they need to practice secrecy, but most important of all, they need to protect themselves from real or imagined persecution.

This is very important for non-Witches to understand. If you say or do anything that appears like you are criticizing

Wicca or Witchcraft, this may be perceived as a personal attack. In other words, be careful when discussing your feelings about Wicca with Witches. If you talk about why Wicca is wrong, or bad, or sinful, or irrational, you will just be alienating your audience. If you start quoting Bible verses to Witches, they will just write you off as a Christian "oppressor."

I'm not saying that Wicca or Witchcraft is above criticism. I don't believe anything is above criticism, including Paganism. However, as a non-Wiccan, you need to understand that the concept of the burning times means that many Witches are especially sensitive when it comes to anything that may be perceived as an attack. If you want to share your concerns, anxieties, or criticisms of Wicca with a Witch you know, make sure you are expressing your viewpoint in the most gentle, thoughtful, nonjudgmental, nonblaming way possible. That's the only way you'll ever get your point across.

Part Three:

Going
Beyond the
Stereotypes

Stereotypes are a major obstacle when it comes to understanding any minority group, culture, or religion. Everyone knows how harmful stereotypes can be and how ugly lies get perpetrated through widely accepted misconceptions. The Pagan community has to contend with inaccurate images, ranging from devil worship to human sacrifice to wanton orgies.

The questions in Part Three attack the stereotypes head on. I set the record straight on a variety of misconceptions, from the seemingly harmless ones (Witches don't have "familiars") to the really damaging ideas (no blood is ever spilled in a Wiccan ritual). If you have a nagging fear that this really is just a front for sexual license or irrational behavior, please read on. Your fears come from stereotyping, and only the facts will lay them to rest.

Why do Witches wear black?

One of the common stereotypes about Witches, both in the past and in the present, is that they love to wear black. From the black robes sported by the wicked Witch in *The Wizard of Oz* or *Snow White and the Seven Dwarves*, to today's teenager whose black clothes are balanced by tattoos and body piercings, the color of the night seems to be the color of choice among Witches.

Like all stereotypes, it's a bit unfair. Yes, I know plenty of Pagans who love to wear black (I'm one of them); but I also know plenty of non-Pagans who like to wear black, so what does it prove? Meanwhile, some of the Witches I know are among the most colorful and stylish of dressers. The Witches who wear black regularly do so for one simple reason: they like the color. They think it looks good on them, or they enjoy dressing in dramatic, mysterious ways. The same goes, incidentally, for tattoos and body piercings. Not all Witches adorn their bodies in this way, and not everyone who wears tattoos or piercings is Pagan.

So just because the teenager in your house likes heavy metal music, has a ring through her nose, and never wears anything lighter than midnight, does not necessarily mean she's a Witch. Likewise, if your teenager starts reading about Witchcraft, that doesn't mean that the wardrobe will suddenly go dark.

The black clothes, tattoos, and body piercings are part of a secular trend in culture known as the Gothic scene.

Gothics (or Goths for short) tend to be intelligent, well-read young people who find enjoyment in dark humor, cynical philosophy, and artforms that explore the darker side of the human experience. Thus, many Goths appreciate horror novels, heavy metal music, and cyberpunk (dark science fiction). Why do Goths have such a fascination with the dark? That's a book all its own. It may be a way to express adolescent anger. It may be an artistic way to express social or political protest. Or it may simply be because it's cool.

Some Goths feel drawn to Wicca because they appreciate the dark irony of a religion that suffered intense persecution in ages past. But some of them might find that excessive cynicism and anti-authoritarianism doesn't really mesh well with the craft, which is much more based on virtues such as love, trust, and healing. Generally speaking, the Goth culture is a bit more chaotic and anti-establishment than is the Wiccan community. Still, many Goths do seem drawn to Wicca, so there is definitely an overlap.

Why were Witches historically depicted wearing black? Black has a long-standing reputation in our society as the color of evil. Because Witches were seen as evil, of course they would be seen as wearing black. But this view is unfair, not only to Witchcraft, but to the color black itself.

Some Witches believe black is a magically neutral color and prefer to wear black when performing their rituals. But this is not the majority view. Most Witches love to wear bright colors when participating in the ceremonies of the old religion.

Do Witches have Familiars?

Another stereotype from olden days involves the notion of the Witch's familiar. This would be an animal, often a cat, that was seen as a demon that took the form of the animal, and lived with the Witch. This demon animal was seen as the Witch's servant, and thus would obey the Witch's command.

Well, many Witches have cats, dogs, ferrets, iguanas, parrots, fish, and various other animals. Witches tend to be nature lovers, and therefore tend to be animal lovers. Maybe Witches have more pets than the national average, but some Witches are allergic to cats, or travel too much to keep a dog, or simply don't want to clean up the mess. So there's no requirement for Witches to keep animals. As for these animals having supernatural powers or abilities: well, sorry to disappoint you, but that just isn't so.

The historical concept of the familiar may actually be connected with Shamanism (see question 55 for more on this topic). Shamanism, the indigenous spiritual practice of tribal cultures, often involves the shaman (medicine man or witchdoctor) using spiritual tools to perform magical rituals. One common tool that shamans use is a process of connecting with the spirits of animals, in order to gain the medicine (spiritual power) of that particular type of animal. Thus, a shaman might go into a trance and, in the spirit world, interact with an elk to gain its medicine. This would then enable the shaman to perform healing rituals for someone who needed elk medicine to survive.

The spirit animals that shamans would interact with are known as power animals. Some scholars believe that Witchcraft is the descendent of European forms of Shamanism. Maybe in ages past, when healers of old would go into their trances and do spiritual work with animal spirits, those healers developed a reputation for having animal spirits to help them heal. Then, when the persecution of Witches began, that concept of the animal spirit transformed into the idea of the familiar.

This is speculation, of course. But it's a reasonable theory as to how the idea of the familiar came about. Today, many Witches are students of Shamanism and are interested in the concept of the power animal. However, when it comes to keeping pets, the only real reason Witches do so is because they love animals so much.

Why are Witches portrayed as stirring a cauldron? What's in the cauldron anyway?

No doubt you have heard the phrase *a Witches' brew*. This idiom expresses any kind of liquid or potion that is noxious, dangerous, toxic, or otherwise unfit for human consumption. When you call something a Witches' brew, you are subconsciously perpetuating our society's bias against Witchcraft. The stereotype involves the image of the Witch creating a potion in her cauldron (seen in movies, cartoons, fairy tales, and in Shakespeare's *Macbeth*). With foul fumes coming off of the contents of the cauldron, one can only assume just how evil the concoction being stirred must be!

Like most stereotypes, this image has some interesting roots in mythology as well as in the tradition of Witch as a village herbalist/healer. In Celtic mythology, the cauldron was considered one of the four chief treasures of the Irish Gods and Goddesses. The cauldron was a symbol of abundance and prosperity. The Dagda, the God who owned the magic cauldron, could feed entire armies with the food he prepared in it. So originally, the cauldron was not a symbol of evil at all, but actually a symbol of profound goodness, similar to the horn of plenty that symbolizes modern Thanksgiving.

No one is sure how the Celtic cauldron became the Witches' cauldron, but we do know that the Witch as an herbalist and healer would have used plants in her medical practice in a variety of ways. These would have included making potions, ointments, salves, and teas. Each of these could have powerful healing properties, depending on the plants used in the recipe. The cauldron would simply be the utensil used in making the ointments, beverages, or brews. Historically speaking, a "Witches' brew" would have been a medical or healing substance, *not* a poison!

But then came the rise of modern science, modern religion, and modern medicine; folk remedies and herbal healing practices fell out of favor. Perhaps one of the ways the establishment attacked the village herbalist was by accusing her recipes of being toxic or dangerous—a "Witches' brew."

In today's practice of Witchcraft, a cauldron is an optional item. Many Witches, especially those who form covens or other groups, like the symbolism of the cauldron as a representation of abundance and prosperity. There are plenty of kitchen Witches practicing their spirituality like the ancient wise women/herbalists, and making folk remedies and herbal salves in their kitchens, who proudly create healing substances. They may be just as likely to use a crockpot as a cauldron. In any event, you can rest assured that the Witches' cauldron, if used at all, is used only to make wholesome, healing recipes.

Do Witches practice animal or human sacrifice?

The answer to this question is a simple and emphatic NO. Witches respect and revere life. To hurt another being, whether animal or human, would be to violate the ethical commandment of Witchcraft "harm none" (see question 34). I think it's unfortunate that I even have to mention this awful subject, but given the kinds of hysterical misinformation that continues to appear in movies and in the media, it's important to be as clear as possible.

Witches and Wiccans do not believe in killing either animals or humans. Period. Naturally, many Witches are meat eaters, and I suppose those who grow their own livestock may slaughter their dinner, just as farmers (of any religion) have done since the dawn of time. But that's not the same thing as a religious ritual of animal sacrifice.

Many Witches are vegetarians, and find the entire notion of blood sacrifice totally creepy and repulsive.

One of the most beautiful writings in the literature of Witchcraft is the *Charge of the Goddess*, written by Doreen Valiente. It includes words that the Goddess speaks to those who revere her. Among other things, she proclaims that she does *not* require sacrifice, for she is the mother of all that lives. For this reason, most Witches would say not only that they don't do sacrifice, but that if anyone did, it would be displeasing to the Goddess.

So why do the stereotypes persist?

Once again, we have Hollywood to thank. We do know that in ancient times, most religions performed animal sacrifices, human sacrifices, or both (the Bible speaks very frankly about the ancient practices of human and animal sacrifice among the Hebrew people). There is evidence that Druids also performed human sacrifice. Because such blood sacrifice is associated with primitive or Pagan religions, and because Witchcraft is inspired by primitive and Pagan religions, you can see where the stereotype originates.

Modern Witches maintain that, just as Judaism and other religions evolved away from blood sacrifice, so has modern Witchcraft. No matter what the ancients of any religious persuasion may have done, today's Witches disavow anything that causes harm.

Are Witches on drugs?

Many Witches love to use fanciful language to describe their spirituality. With all the talk about magic, fairies, reincarnation, rituals, and other unusual and out of the ordinary things that seem to be part of the Wiccan world, a non-Witch might come to the conclusion that practitioners of the old religion are all addicted to hallucinogenic drugs. Ever since the days of the Beatles, LSD and meditation seemed to go hand in hand. And many Pagans have a libertarian, live-and-let-live attitude toward life. In that context, one might assume that drug use and addiction could be rampant.

Pagans and Witches are no more likely to abuse drugs than any other segment of society. I can only speak from personal observation (to the best of my knowledge no one has done any research on Pagans and drug abuse), but my sense is that Witches are no more, or less, likely to use or abuse drugs than anyone else.

Like many churches, Pagan organizations often have rules governing the use of alcohol and other drugs. At a minimum, Pagan groups enforce the law and prohibit the use of illegal drugs altogether. Among Pagan adults, alcohol use is generally tolerated, but only in moderation. Most groups have rules prohibiting the use of alcohol or even milder drugs like caffeine when participating in a Pagan ritual. The use of mind-altering substances is seen as a detriment to the full experience of the ritual's magic.

You may run across Pagan individuals with drug or alcohol problems; if so, remember that the addiction is not caused by Pagan beliefs. Nothing in the Pagan or Wiccan religion requires or encourages a person to use drugs, drink, or otherwise abuse substances. Most Pagans and Witches are committed to sobriety. A person with a substance abuse problem can overcome their addiction and remain a dedicated Pagan. In fact, since Paganism encourages values such as love, trust, and non-harm, many people may find that the old religion helps them to become or stay sober.

Pagans, like liberal Christians, tend to be tolerant of alcohol use, so it is possible to encounter "party Pagans" whose use of alcohol is exuberant, if not excessive. And although I have never seen it, I suppose it is possible that some Pagan groups may, as a group, be engaged in patterns of drug abuse.

But a group with this kind of problem is not representative of Paganism or Witchcraft as a whole. Most Pagan groups and individuals have mature, responsible, law-abiding attitudes toward alcohol and drugs.

Do Witches have orgies?

One of the most salacious of rumors to swirl around Paganism and Witchcraft, dating all the way back to the burning times, is the idea that Witches have orgies.

During the burning times, the lurid depictions of Witches' gatherings would include descriptions of the leaders extinguishing the lights and then everybody grabbing the person next to them to engage in acts of carnal lust, regardless of that person's age or gender. Most historians today believe these descriptions tell us more about the kinky fantasies of the people who persecuted the alleged Witches than about "Witchcraft" itself. But whatever their origin, these allegations of bisexual orgies in the dark have given Witchcraft a naughty reputation that remains with it to this day.

Other factors contribute to the sex-Witchcraft connection. As explained below, some traditions of Witchcraft practice their rituals in the nude. Among many Wiccan and other Pagan groups, themes of fertility play a central role in the spirituality of the old religion. Generally speaking, Witches and Pagans have a positive attitude toward sexuality, seeing it as a gift from the Goddess, and therefore not fraught with the sinful dangers that other religions see in sex. Some

Wiccan groups have a ritual called "the Great Rite," which involves a symbolic enactment of the sex act between the priest and priestess officiating the ritual. Some Wiccan groups even go so far as to perform rituals in which the Great Rite involves actual sexual intercourse.

To the average American who has grown up in a world full of problems such as sexual abuse, incest, rape, and degrading pornography, a religion that is sex-positive or that has a tradition of sexually-inspired rituals may seem threatening or dangerous. But Wiccans are like everyone else in their opposition to sexual misconduct. Where Witches differ from society as a whole is that Witches believe if religion were more sexy in healthy and loving ways, our society would be less plagued by problems of sexual abuse or misconduct.

Witches do have generally liberal attitudes toward sex, and Witchcraft does include fertility symbolism and the positive erotic symbolism of the Great Rite. But that's as far as it goes. Witches do not engage in orgies, group sex, anonymous sex, or anything else that would imply promiscuous debauchery. Witches do not condone rape, sex with children, or any form of coercive or non-consensual sexual act. Indeed, because so many Witches are feminist or pro-feminist, they tend to see the goodness of sex only in ways that are safe and comfortable, especially for women.

There are a few ways in which the Pagan community is noticeably more liberal than society as a whole when it comes to sex. Most Pagans accept gay and lesbian sexuality and have no problem with gay or lesbian couples. For this reason, most Pagans also accept sexual relationships that do not include marriage. Still, most Pagans who form committed relationships do get married, a practice that Pagans call "handfasting." Handfasting may or may not include a legal (state-sanctioned) marriage. For example, many gay or lesbian Wiccans will be handfasted in a Pagan ritual, but their commitment is not recognized by the government. Still, to Pagans, it is considered a sacred and binding union.

An even smaller segment of the Pagan community engages in sexually open relationships. This is true of society as a whole. Since the sexual revolution of the 1960s and 1970s, a small segment of society has engaged in "swinging," or the practice of couples having sex with multiple partners. A more recent concept, "polyamory," involves people who form loving relationships (which may or may not be sexual) with more than one partner. These avant-garde practices are not inherently Pagan or Wiccan; but because Paganism in general is so positive in its approach to sex, some Pagans and Wiccans do participate in these lifestyles without any religious guilt or shame. But even within the Pagan community, they remain in the minority. Most Pagans confine their sexual activity to adults in committed relationships with one other person.

Do Witches do their rituals in the nude?

Some do. But many do not.

Over the centuries, artists have portrayed Witches performing their rituals in the nude. This was one aspect of the old religion that Gerald Gardner heartily endorsed (Gardner, it seems, was a nudist before he became a Wiccan). Gardner wrote that Witches had a word, "skyclad," to describe the practice of ritual nudity. Many of the covens and other Pagan groups in Gardner's lineage, or similar traditions, still practice ritual nudity all or part of the time. Many other groups have a "clothing optional" policy, where ritual participants can choose whether or not to wear clothing in rituals.

Today, most historians of Paganism and Witchcraft scoff at the idea of there being a long tradition of ritual nudity among Witches. Remember, Gardner was British; the damp and cold British climate is hardly conducive to outdoor nudity! Many traditional Wiccan groups insist that wearing robes is the more "authentic" practice. Be that as it may, nearly all Witches and Pagans perform their rituals wearing either a robe or some other specially made garment, or simply wear ordinary clothes. Skyclad covens seem to be in the minority.

Those Witches who do perform rituals skyclad see it as a way of creating a spirit of equality. Everyone is equal when they're naked. Also, the emphasis is on trust and openness, *not* on sex. After all, most human beings do not have a "Playboy" or "*GQ*" body, so a group full of normal, ordinary naked people is hardly a hothouse of lustful desire. Instead, skyclad Witches see their nudity as a symbolic way to become *psychologically* naked, which is the best mental state for participating in a ritual. Even Witches who wear robes in their ritual often try to cultivate a similar sense of psychological openness and trust.

If the idea of getting naked in a ritual bothers you, remember that most Witches don't do it. Even among those who do, the emphasis is not on sexuality. People who are naturally modest or uncomfortable with nudity can find plenty of Wiccan groups where robes are always worn in ritual.

Are Witches Kinky?

According to the rumors, Witches are into whips, bondage, and other kinds of alternative practices. The truth is not nearly as exciting as the rumor. In a small percentage of Wiccan traditions, a ritual whip (scourge) is used, not for sexual purposes, but strictly as part of the Witches' religious ceremonies. As for bondage, some groups will use blindfolds or restraints in initiation rituals (ceremonies in which individuals are welcomed into the practice of Witchcraft or are elevated into positions of leadership within the coven). Again, however, these practices are not universal, and when they are used, it is always within a safe and structured ceremonial setting, never for sexual purposes. Wiccans and other Pagans seek to have meaningful spiritual experiences in their rituals, but the ceremonies are always designed to be structured and safe.

The idea that Witches are kinky probably comes from the use of the scourge. This is mainly a practice of Gardnerian Witches, although some other traditionalist groups use the ritual whip as well. In ritual, it is used in a very dignified and elegant manner, its purpose being to symbolize the importance of spiritual intent over physical comfort. Many Wiccan groups feel the scourge is not particularly useful, and don't use it in ritual at all. Others, trying to keep traditional practices alive, do use it. However, controversy surrounds just how traditional this aspect of Wiccan ritual really is. At least one historian has speculated that Gardner himself had a sexual obsession with whips, and basically wrote them into the rituals of his coven because they turned him on. Of course, Gardner is long dead, and is unavailable to comment one way or the other. By now, the question is moot. Many Wiccans don't use the scourge at all; and those that do, use it in a dignified ceremonial manner.

Is Witchcraft irrational?

Non-Pagans with a scientific or rationalist mind may suspect that Witchcraft, whatever its moral qualities, is hopelessly out of touch with the real world. It is indeed a tradition that is based on ancient ideas, romantic myths, seemingly impractical pursuits such as magic and ritual, and a willingness to believe in such fantastic notions as the existence of fairies or the idea that the Earth as a whole is a living, conscious entity.

Science-minded people who see the world in Newtonian terms (in other words, as a giant, lifeless machine) may well draw the conclusion that Paganism is unscientific. But for those who are willing to entertain the magic and mystery of modern/quantum physics, the distinction between "rationalistic" and "religious" becomes blurred. Modern physics does not see the universe as some sort of inert machine, but more as an incredibly complex pattern of dancing energies. In this world, the distinctions between matter and energy, or between mind and body, or even between the soul and physical existence, all become blurred. In the world of cutting edge science, what may appear irrational to a Newtonian physicist suddenly seems not so far out after all.

Paganism and Wicca rely on several basic assumptions, such as the following:

- ✪ That the universe we live in has a basic quality of consciousness.

- ✪ That the human mind can actually shape or impact its material surroundings.

- ✪ That dreams, random events, and the cycles of the physical world all have meaning that can be understood in a spiritual way.

To the strictly rational mind, these assumptions may seem unprovable, and therefore not worthy of serious intellectual pursuit. But Wiccans and Pagans see it the other way around. These kinds of assumptions cannot be disproven, and therefore they are fair game for a curious person to explore, at least on a spiritual level. That is the intellectual foundation of nature spirituality.

While many Witches and other Pagans love mythology, and see the natural world as a magical place populated by fairies, Goddesses, and other spirit beings, it is not a requirement for Pagans to believe in mythology. Indeed, people with a strong scientific mind but who want a nature-oriented spirituality can feel comfortable within Wicca, accepting the mythology as a charming fantasy. Because Paganism stresses the importance of following your individual conscience in spiritual matters, there is room in the Wiccan community for both skeptics and true believers.

The rationale of Wicca may not include the brilliant, airtight logic of a Vulcan philosopher, but neither is it entirely irrational. To anyone who is willing to say "maybe" to the basic assumptions of the old religion, it all makes sense.

Part Four:

What Do Witches Believe?

The last section explained what isn't true about the Pagan path. Now it's time to look at nature spirituality in a positive light. What do Witches believe, what do they think, what spiritual and philosophical ideas are important to them? The questions in Part Four will help you to understand the basic principles of Paganism.

Here you'll learn more about Goddess spirituality, the Wiccan Rede (the rule of ethics for Witches), the importance of nature in Paganism, and Wiccan views regarding life after death. A basic book like this cannot provide a comprehensive introduction to Wiccan thought, but hopefully you'll come away from this section with a better understanding of the basics.

Why do Witches place so much emphasis on the Goddess?

To people raised in traditional religions such as Christianity, Judaism, or Islam, the concept of the Goddess may be one of the most unusual, and perhaps even threatening, characteristics of Wicca and Paganism.

After all, the "big three" religions have consistently seen God in masculine terms. God is seen as a *he*. Indeed, since the feminine form is God*dess*, to call the Supreme Being God in itself implies a masculine gender for Spirit.

Liberals within Christianity or Judaism sometimes assert that, technically speaking, God is beyond gender: neither male nor female, or maybe encompassing both genders. But what is technically true on a philosophical or theological level does not really translate into daily practice. For most people, God is a "he," plain and simple. A statement like "Since God loves us, we know she is good" sounds silly.

Witches and Pagans question this way of seeing things. Why should God be just a guy? The Bible says that God "created man in his own image" (Genesis 1:27). Well, what about woman? Are we to assume that women are therefore inferior to men, since men are more consistent with the image of God than women (don't laugh, this argument has been made before)? Or maybe this male-God is simply a human construct. Instead of God creating man in his own image, maybe it was the *men* who created God in *their* own image! Indeed, many Pagans would say this is so.

To say that the Supreme Spirit only embodies one gender is to exclude 50 percent of the population from having a spiritual link to the Divine. Pagans and Witches prefer to see God as both a female Goddess and a male God, who are united in their love for one another.

But what about monotheism? Many Witches see God and Goddess as two halves of a single whole. Just as Christians see the Father, the Son, and the Holy Ghost as three aspects of a single God, so do many Witches regard God and Goddess as two aspects of a single Spirit. You can be a monotheist and still think in terms of Goddess and God.

So why do Witches place so much emphasis on the Goddess? Because it seems only fair. For many Witches, emphasizing the Goddess over the God is a way to redress the imbalance of the mainstream religions, where Goddess energy is not present at all. Other Witches strive to honor God and Goddess equally. Still, to someone unfamiliar with the concept of the Goddess, it may seem that Witches overemphasize it, just because is the Goddess seems so unusual.

To Witches and other Pagans, honoring the Goddess is just part of honoring nature. Since it is natural for human beings to be both male and female, it's only natural for Spirit to be the same.

Why do Witches place so much emphasis on nature?

Witches might respond to this question with a question of their own: "Why do other religions place so much emphasis on a book?" From the Jewish Torah, to the Christian New Testament, to the Muslim Qu'ran, to the Hindu Vedas, to the Buddhist Dhammapada, religion after religion is bound up in some sort of collection of sacred writings.

These books are printed on paper, which is made from trees. Witches prefer to learn from the trees while they're still alive in the forest.

Witchcraft and Paganism are spiritual paths rooted in love and reverence for nature. This can be compared, roughly, to the love and devotion that other religions show to their sacred writings. But where Christians call the Bible the "Word of God," Witches see nature in a more intimate way: as the body of the Goddess.

Most people think of living beings as consisting of a body and a soul. The soul is the part that actually animates the body, the part that most religious and spiritual people believe is immortal, unlike the body, which will eventually die and decay. Every human soul has a body in which it lives and functions. But what is the body of God (or the Goddess)? Mainstream religion never really asks this question, and so it appears that God is really just some sort of disembodied mind.

But what if the entire physical universe were the "body" of God?

Not all Witches may see it precisely this way, but I suspect many would say this idea makes sense. Just as the human soul resides in a human body, so the soul of the God and the Goddess reside in the physical universe. In other words, in nature.

Nature is more than just the wilderness. Nature basically includes all that physically exists, from the densest matter up to the most ethereal energy. Many religions see the natural world as somehow separate from God, and some religions even see it as "fallen" or "sinful." Not Wicca. To Witches, the physical dimension of existence is just as sacred and holy as the spiritual dimension. This means that the human body is just as good as the soul. And the natural universe is just as good and worthy as the realm of Spirit.

Many Witches believe it is a philosophical error to see the Spiritual realm as somehow more good or pure than the material realm. Instead, the Pagan traditions regard both matter and spirit as equally good, but different, and therefore to be experienced or related to in different ways. But neither one is better than the other.

Pagans emphasize nature because they believe it is good. They believe nature is a profound and wise teacher. And they believe nature is beautiful and nurturing. Sure, our natural bodies eventually die and decay. But that is the natural rhythm of things. Witches have an optimistic view of life after death (see question 35), and are able to accept even the sad aspects of the natural world.

Why is mythology so important to Witches?

I've talked about how Witches prefer to turn to nature rather than to a book as their source of inspiration. But this doesn't mean that Witches are opposed to human wisdom or to the knowledge that can be gained from the written word. Indeed, many Witches have found that mythology, or the sacred stories from cultures the world over, have been a powerful source of information and inspiration on their spiritual path.

Many people consider mythology to be just a collection of fables. The stories of Gods and Goddesses such as Zeus, Aphrodite and Apollo are about as believable as tales of Santa Claus or the Tooth Fairy. Our society has a bias, that if a story isn't "true," then it somehow isn't important.

Ironically, many scholars believe the Bible is filled with myths, stories filled with spiritual symbolism but without any authentic historical content. From the creation of the universe taking only seven days to Jonah's three-day excursion in the belly of a whale, to Jesus walking on water and feeding thousands of people with just a few loaves and fishes, story after story in the Bible has a mythological feel. Some people, even many liberal Christians, accept that the Bible is full of myth. But many conservative Christians insist that the Bible must be read as literally, infallibly true. This seems to say more about their insecurities than about spiritual truth.

What the liberal Christians and Pagans have in common is a recognition that myth can teach us spiritual truths regardless of whether it is literally or historically factual. Most Witches could care less if Persephone and Dionysus are "real" figures. The spiritual truths that can be found in their myths are meaningful whether or not the myths have a basis in factual history.

Many theories exist about the nature and history of mythology. One theory suggests that myths originated as tales told about ancestors, that over time became embellished with supernatural flourishes until the ancestors were regarded as Gods and Goddesses. Different Pagans and Witches will have different theories about the nature and purpose of mythology. But what Witches share in common is a recognition that myths can teach important spiritual truths, as embodied in the various Gods, Goddesses, heroes, and heroines who appear in mythology.

Some Witches and Pagans restrict themselves to the myths from only one culture, such as Egyptian myth or Celtic myth. Others read and study myths from around the world. There is no one right way to approach the study of mythology. Each Wiccan individual or group chooses for themselves which myths to read and study.

Are Witches polytheists?

If Witches believe in both the Goddess and the God, and if Witches study various myths with many different Gods and Goddesses in them, it may seem that Witches believe in and worship many different deities, instead of the one Supreme Being that monotheists acknowledge.

This is not as easy a question as it may appear on the surface. To say "either you're a monotheist or a polytheist" is to regard the world very simplistically. For example, many Christians believe in a Father, Son, and Holy Spirit, but also insist they're monotheists. This is because the Father, Son, and Holy Spirit are three elements or aspects of a single unified God. Others, such as Jews or Muslims, may disagree with the Christians, but for Christians it's important to believe in this three-in-one (or "trinity") God.

For Pagans and Witches, the distinction between monotheism and polytheism is a lot like this Christian concept of the trinity. Wiccans will talk about Aphrodite and Artemis and Athena like they are three entirely different Goddesses. But then they will talk about *"the* Goddess," which implies only one Goddess. Indeed, some Wiccan groups teach "All Goddesses are one Goddess, and all Gods are one God" as a way of maintaining a monotheistic perspective. Since the Goddess and the God are two aspects of a single Ultimate Spirit, to say all Goddesses are one Goddess and all Gods are one God is to say that all mythological deities are aspects of a single Spirit, kind of like different facets on a single diamond.

Here is where it gets tricky. Some Pagans really are more comfortable with a polytheistic perspective. They say, "I prefer to see the universe run by a committee rather than by a dictator." This is a minority position among Pagans, but it does exist.

Then again, many Pagans would ultimately say that it doesn't matter if they are polytheists or monotheists. The myths are just myths, symbolic stories designed to impart spiritual truths. But the real important thing is nature, which is both unified (there is one universe) and infinitely diverse (think of all the countless varieties of life forms).

So in the end, there's no easy way to answer this question. Many Witches would prefer to identify themselves as monotheistic, but with a clear understanding that Spirit includes both Goddess and God aspects, and that these aspects can be understood through a variety of mythological Gods and Goddesses. Other Witches may be more comfortable regarding themselves as polytheists.

Are Witches pantheists or animists?

A pantheist is a person who believes everything is God. An animist is a person who believes that everything has a spirit, although not all spirits are necessarily unified in a single God. There are indeed elements of pantheism and animism within Wicca.

As we saw in the answer to question 29, many Witches are comfortable with the idea that the universe, or nature, can be regarded as the "body" of the Goddess. Some would not even make that distinction, but would simply say the universe *is* the Goddess. This is pretty much a pantheist perspective.

Incidentally, another concept, similar but not identical to pantheism, sees the universe as existing within God, but that God is still somehow larger or greater than the universe. This is called *panentheism*. Actually, many Witches are panentheists rather than pantheists, since Witches often see the Goddess as having a spiritual dimension above and beyond the physical universe. But all of this is philosophical hairsplitting. Different Witches have many different ways of thinking about the universe, but not everyone would agree with these statements.

The main implication of pantheism or panentheism is that the physical universe, or nature, are therefore seen as part of God (or the Goddess), and therefore are seen as good. This is certainly true for Witches, who regard the physical nature of things as sacred.

Animism sees various individual things as having animating spirits. Each tree, animal, rock, river, stream, and so forth all have their own unique spirits. Many primitive Pagan cultures (such as the ancient Celts) were animistic. Animism is different from pantheism because, instead of seeing all material things as being part of a single supreme being, animism sees different things as having different spirits. In this way, animism is more polytheistic than monotheistic.

Some Pagans do regard various physical objects as having a spirit, and thus are animistic. Many Pagans regard living things such as trees or plants or animals as having powerful spirits who can guide or teach them. Others believe in spirits associated with rivers, rocks, mountains, and storms. However, not all Pagans are oriented toward seeing nature in this way. And many of the Pagans who do see the world in an animistic way still believe in one over-arching God/Goddess Spirit. So the smaller animistic spirits are seen as part of the supreme Spirit, as a drop of water is part of the ocean.

Many Witches and Pagans grow impatient with academic or philosophical categories such as polytheism, pantheism, animism, or panentheism. To many Witches, these are abstract terms with little bearing on real-world spirituality. Such Witches are less concerned with beliefs and much more focused on experience. The experience of Wicca, to them, is where spiritual power can be found. The philosophical label you use to describe yourself isn't seen as that important.

Why do Witches call the God "the Horned One"?

Some Witches and other Pagans refer to the masculine aspect of God as *the Horned God* or *the Horned One*. This can be alarming to Christians or others who mistakenly assume they are referring to Satan. After all, Satan is typically portrayed as being a red-skinned human-like being with cloven hooves for feet, a long pointed tail, and two prominent horns on the brow of his head. If the devil has horns, and the Pagan God has horns, well... .

But don't jump to conclusions here. There is the question of who came first: the Pagan God, or the Christian devil. The idea of a God with horns is actually quite ancient, and pre-dates the coming of Christianity by thousands of years. In various cultures, different mythological Gods have been depicted as having horns. Cernunnos, the Celtic horned God (indeed, his name means "horned one") is depicted as a Lord of the forest and the animals. In a similar way, the Greek God Pan is depicted as having horns and goat-like legs and feet. Like Cernunnos, Pan is seen as a God of nature and of wild beasts.

The reason these Gods have horns is simple: many male animals have horns (or antlers), and so horns are a profound symbol of masculinity. To Pagans, they are symbols of the inherent relationship between nature and the masculine face of God.

So how did the horned God come to be regarded as evil? In Christian symbolism, what better way to depict the cosmic bad guy than by drawing imagery from the Gods of the old religion that Christianity was competing against? When Christian writers and artists from centuries past sought to describe Satan, they drew inspiration from the old Pagan Gods such as Pan and Cernunnos. Because the Pagan Gods had horns, Satan ended up being depicted with horns as well.

Once again, let me repeat the most essential message of this book: Witches, Wiccans, and Pagans do not worship the devil. Christians borrowed the horned symbolism from Paganism to illustrate the thoroughly Christian concept of Satan. To Pagans, both in ancient times and today, the horns of the horned God are not symbols of evil, but of life and vibrant, healthy masculinity.

Do Witches have a moral code?

Yes. An elegantly simple, and surprisingly demanding, moral code. It is summed up in only one single, focused statement, called the Wiccan Rede. "Rede" is an archaic English word for "standard." At only eight short words long, the Rede is simple enough for a child to memorize, and yet profound enough to keep a philosopher wrestling with its implications for a lifetime.

Several versions of the Rede exist, all slightly different because of the use of archaic language. But in modern English the Wiccan Rede goes like this: *If it harms none, do what you will.*

On the surface, it's simple enough. It makes a positive statement for personal freedom, as long as your actions do not infringe on someone else. But then, on reflection, it becomes clear what a demanding code this is. Harm *none*. That includes yourself. Self-destructive or self-sabotaging behaviors are out. What does this say about military service, self-defense, or capital punishment? Does it extend to non-humans, implying the necessity of a meatless diet? Also, the prohibition of harm involves more than just physical harm; it includes emotional or psychological harm. Thus, adultery and lying are just as prohibited as are murder and rape.

These questions have provoked vibrant and ongoing debate within the Pagan community. Needless to say, differing opinions exist. Some Pagans are strict in their interpretation of the Wiccan Rede, adopting an almost Buddha-like commitment to nonviolence, vegetarianism, and pacifism. Others, however, take a much more pragmatic approach, seeing the Rede as an ethical ideal that does not apply to military service. Some Wiccan groups have even adopted a version of the Wiccan Rede that says, "If it harms none, do what you will, unless in your own self-defense." Despite these differing philosophical positions, the main idea of the Wiccan Rede remains constant: to follow the path of Witchcraft is to make a sacred commitment to harming none.

Another ethical teaching common among Witches is the "Threefold Law," which suggests that any energy a Witch puts out into the world will come back to him or her three times amplified. If a Witch commits an act of kindness, or performs a spell of healing, he or she will eventually have that same kindness or healing work repaid in some form three times over. Likewise, any negative act performed will result in a payback three times as bad as the initial act. Basically, this is a law of investment and return. Invest good actions and energy into your environment, and you will receive a threefold blessing. But invest negativity, and you will suffer accordingly. It's a practical concept that functions as both incentive to behave ethically and a caution against harmful acts.

What do Witches believe happens after we die?

Like most spiritual people, Witches believe in the immortality of the soul. The body is left to return to the earth at the point of death, but a person's spirit lives on.

However, few (if any) Witches believe in the concepts of judgment, heaven, or hell. To most Pagans, this way of seeing life after death is overly simplistic, based on an immature longing for all things to be easily categorized as good or bad. In truth, every human being is a complex and profound mixture of saint and sinner. For this reason, most Pagans tend to be more comfortable with the Eastern concepts of karma and reincarnation as explanations of the soul's fate after death.

Reincarnation may be thought of as the recycling of souls. We know that the physical dimension of life—our bodies— are "recycled" after death, as the water, salt, carbon, and other minerals and elements in our bodies return to the environment. Why wouldn't the same process apply to our souls? Instead of going for eternity in paradise or perdition, reincarnation suggests that a soul, after a period of renewal in an otherworldly abode, returns to the Earth (or maybe some other planet in the physical universe) to experience the joys and sorrows of life yet again.

Karma involves the concept of cause and effect. It is the ultimate law of justice that governs all things in the universe. Every person has karma, based on the sum total of their actions—good, bad, or ambiguous. Karma shapes what happens to a person, both in the life currently being lived as well as in future incarnations. Karma means that each person is responsible for the circumstances of his or her life. This responsibility is not meant to blame the victim, as if poor or handicapped people deserve their suffering. But rather it means that each person can take responsibility for whatever the circumstances of their life may be, positive or negative. By responding in positive ways, they can create good karma for themselves, which will result in improved life circumstances, either in this life or in a future incarnation.

What happens in between incarnations? Most religious traditions throughout the world speak of some sort of otherworldly paradise or place of rest where souls return after death. In Welsh mythology, this place is called the Summerland. To Witches, the Summerland is a beautiful place of joy, feasting, and deep rest and renewal. It is a place where a soul can reflect on the life just lived, and prepare for the next incarnation to come.

Incidentally, some spiritual traditions see the world we live in as a dreary place full of suffering, and reincarnation as little more than a curse that souls must suffer through until they can finally scrape together enough good karma to be enlightened, and thereby escape the wheel of rebirth. Witches generally have a more optimistic view of life. Rebirth after rebirth is not a burden to escape, but a process in which we can learn to find joy, meaning, and most of all, love. To Witches, the truth feels good; so finding the truth about the world we live in means finding joy and happiness, life after life after life.

Do Witches believe in evil?

We live in a world where bad things happen. If there is no devil, then why does evil exist? Even after 2,000 years and generations of brilliant philosophers and theologians, Christianity has not yet figured out the problem of evil. So I certainly can't do this topic justice in this book. Let's just say that Wiccans acknowledge the existence of evil not as an intelligence, but as an impersonal force of destruction and negativity.

There are two ways to approach the question of evil: through philosophy, and through action. Wiccans and Pagans tend not to be concerned about the philosophy. Most Wiccans would rather take a practical approach. Practically speaking, the issue is not whether evil exists. Everyone knows that suffering and death are part of life. The practical question is, what do we do about it? How do we respond to pain, illness, and suffering when they occur? To Wiccans, the answer involves healing. Rather than waste time trying to intellectually understand a philosophical mystery, many Witches prefer to take the active, practical approach and dedicate themselves to healing work in some form. Healing means not only trying to alleviate suffering once it occurs, but also trying to create a healthy and balanced society where suffering and evil are prevented from occurring.

The philosophy of evil is linked to the belief in the devil. As I've already said more than once, Witches reject the idea that a purely malevolent being exists who is dedicated to spreading evil. For Witches, spirituality is not about resisting the temptations of the devil. Instead, many Witches would say that their spiritual path involves working to *heal* the problems of illness, sickness, and brokenness, for whatever reason they occur. Witches tend to emphasize healing over worrying about the causes of evil. Rather than arguing over what causes bad things to happen, Pagans would rather just focus on creating more good through healing, prevention, and love.

Part Five:

What Do
Witches Do?

Many Witches and other Pagans will tell you that what they believe is not as important as what they experience. In other words, this is a religious/spiritual path of action instead of mere philosophy. So an important step toward understanding nature spirituality is learning about the activities and practices that are central to it.

In this section you'll learn why Witches love Halloween and the full moon, just what a ritual is, and how a coven (group of Witches) is organized. Some of the terms and ideas may be a bit unfamiliar, but as you read through, you'll see that the craft is simply another way of being religious, not as popular or widely accepted as Christianity or Judaism, but meaningful and positive for those who choose it.

What are the main activities of Witchcraft?

When people become Witches, how do they practice their spirituality? Wicca is considered a craft of the wise. It involves the pursuit of wisdom in many forms. Thus, people who explore the old religion will do any or all of the following:

- **Study.** Witches often love to read, and many long-time practitioners of the craft have houses crammed full of books. Nowadays, this love of research also extends to the Internet, where countless Websites provide information on mythology, ritual, Goddess lore, and magic.

- **Ritual.** This would be the closest equivalent to going to church or synagogue. Rituals can be performed alone, in small groups, or in larger gatherings. As a general rule, they are performed on the night of the full moon, new moon, or on one of eight special Pagan holidays known as Sabbats (see questions 41 and 42 for more about the Sabbats).

- **Magic.** Less formalized than a ritual, magic consists of any activity aimed at channelling spiritual energy to achieve a specific goal. This can be as simple as meditating before a lit candle or as complex as an intricate ritual involving a series of carefully prepared symbolic objects (see questions 48–52 for more on magic). Incidentally, the process of doing a magical working is known as casting a spell.

✪ **Craft activities.** Many Wiccans and Pagans love to make candles, incense, oils, salves, herbal tinctures, and other items, imbued with natural ingredients that have spiritual significance. Such items are created only for positive magical or healing purposes, and are often used in spells or rituals.

✪ **Nature-based activities.** From planting an herb garden to helping clean up a polluted river, to simply enjoying long walks in the woods, nearly all Witches and Pagans truly love the outdoors. To Pagans, such ecological activities as recycling or composting are not just good civic duties; they are also spiritually sacred acts.

✪ **Other activities designed for spiritual growth.** These miscellaneous pursuits can include meditation, studying a divination system such as astrology or Tarot, taking classes to develop psychic or intuitive ability, or making pilgrimages to ancient sacred sites such as Stonehenge in England or Newgrange in Ireland. Because Witches and Pagans regard all of life as sacred, any of these activities can be spiritually meaningful and an important part of their overall religious observance.

There's no one right way to be a Witch, and so not all Wiccans will do all of these things. But this variety of activities shows the richness and depth of spirituality that is available to modern Pagans.

Can a person be a solitary Witch, or must they work in covens?

It is possible for a Witch to be solitary, although many Pagans find meaning and joy in sharing their spirituality with others.

Witches find inspiration in the ancient spiritual practice of the shaman who served a tribe or village with magical and healing abilities. Shamanism is one of the world's oldest spiritual practices, originating in tribal, hunter-gatherer cultures. Shamans did not organize into religious bodies, but rather worked alone, almost like "spiritual entrepreneurs." In more recent centuries, even after the coming of the Christian religion, many towns and villages in Europe had one or more wisdomkeepers (often called "cunning men" or "cunning women") who were knowledgeable about herbalism, folk remedies, and spiritual wisdom. They served as healers and counselors to the common people of the village. Indeed, modern Wicca considers itself to be the descendent of both Shamanism and the cunning woman/cunning man tradition.

Since those spiritual figures tended to work as solitaries, modern Pagans honor solitary practice as a valid way to express one's spirituality. Other religions, such as Christianity, consider it improper for members of the religion to pursue spirituality without joining a church or other community (like a monastery). But in Wicca, going it solo is perfectly acceptable. For many modern Witches, especially in rural areas, this is also a matter of practicality as they may not have access to a Pagan group nearby.

Though it's perfectly acceptable and preferable for some Witches to work alone, many others prefer the fellowship and educational opportunities that can only be found in a group setting. Wiccan groups go by many names, including covens (the traditional word for a group of Witches), groves, circles, and even churches. There are no rules governing the sizes of such groups. Covens and circles tend to be smaller groups (two to 13 members) while groves and churches tend to be larger. Nowadays, some Wiccan groups are as large as small Christian churches, with 50 to more than 100 members.

Joining a Wiccan coven or grove means meeting others with similar spiritual beliefs, having access to classes or training in magic and ritual, and participating in moving and powerful rituals led by experienced Pagan elders. Meanwhile, like joining any other group, the organization will require financial support, volunteer time, and can sometimes have expectations about members' spiritual practices (for example, some covens ask members not to participate in other Pagan groups outside their own). For these reasons, some Pagans always will find solitary practice more to their liking. To be a solitary Witch or to participate in a group, ultimately, is a matter of personal preference.

What is initiation? What is the difference between the three degrees?

Many, but not all, Wiccan groups have a structured program for learning the entirety of Wiccan philosophy, practice, ritual, and magic. In its most traditional form, this program resembles the process of joining a Masonic lodge. A new-comer goes through a series of initiations. An initiation is a ritual that confers membership within the group, and/or spiritual rights and privileges within the group. Many covens believe initiation confers special spiritual experiences as well. Each level of initiation requires a period of study and prepa-ration before the candidate is deemed ready. Each coven or group has its own unique program of initiation(s).

Here is what one program of initiation might look like. It involves seven distinct stages:

1. A person new to the coven or group would be a *guest*. Generally, guests are welcome only at cer-tain rituals or meetings that have been designed specifically to welcome newcomers.

2. If someone becomes interested in pursuing mem-bership in the coven, he or she would speak to the High Priestess or Priest. If accepted, they become students of the coven, and sometimes would un-dergo a brief ritual of dedication. At this point they are called *neophytes*.

3. The neophyte must study at least a year and a day, sometimes longer, before being ready for initiation. The initiation process involves study, participation in classes and rituals, and involvement in the fel-lowship and work activities of the coven. A candi-date for initiation needs to demonstrate maturity and willingness to be a team player in the group's activities. When ready, the neophyte requests ini-tiation and then goes through a secret ceremony, which often involves making an oath of loyalty to the Goddess and the God. This elevates him or

her to the level of *first degree*. In most covens, a person does not earn the right to be called a Witch until they receive their first degree. First degree initiates can assist in rituals and classes and participate in the rituals and classes that are not open to the public.

4. First degree initiates continue their studies and involvement in the group's activities. Again, a minimum period of a year and a day must pass before the initiate will be eligible for the *second degree*. Once again, this involves a secret initiation ceremony and another oath, which may be to the coven itself and to the tradition of the coven. Second degree initiates are eligible to lead rituals and teach classes, and in some groups are qualified to start their own covens with supervision.

5. The process of studying for the *third degree* involves learning the administrative and leadership skills necessary to run a coven or grove. Once again, it's a minimum of a year and a day (if not longer) of study and preparation before receiving this highest level of initiation. In most groups, third degree Witches are qualified to leave their coven and start their own group, a process known as hiving. Whether they do this or not, third degree initiates are respected as leaders within their community.

6. Not all third degree Wiccans necessarily start their own covens, or take over the top leadership position within their existing group. Those who do receive the special titles of *High Priestess* or *High Priest*. In some traditions, a coven must have a

High Priestess but may or may not require a High Priest. The High Priestess and Priest are the spiritual leaders of the community, and function like the ordained ministers of any other religion. They can officiate at weddings and funerals, and have privileges to visit their spiritual charges when in prison or a hospital.

7. Finally, third degree initiates and High Priestesses and Priests eventually retire from their day-to-day activities leading their covens. At this point, they can assume the title of *elder*. Elders are respected for their wisdom and longstanding experience and knowledge within the community. Even though they may not have official standings within a coven or grove, they are relied on as consultants and mentors to the current leadership.

Different traditions may use these terms in slightly different ways. In some traditions, a person can assume the title of priest or priestess after their first degree initiation, while others require them to receive their third degree before assuming such a title. Meanwhile, other groups may only have one level of initiation, or no initiation at all (especially among Wiccan groups with a strong feminist orientation, the degree system is seen as hierarchical and based in patriarchal thinking).

Do Witches worship the moon?

It might appear as if Wiccans and other Pagans worship the moon, since many rituals occur according to the phases of the moon. The *Charge of the Goddess*, an important traditional Wiccan document, instructs Witches to gather once a month, ideally when the moon is full. Next to the full moon, the next most popular time to gather is during the new moon. Why do Witches place such importance on the lunar phases?

Many mythological traditions identify the moon as a feminine counterpart to the masculine sun. For this reason, a number of Goddesses are associated with the moon, including Artemis or Diana, Selena, and of course, Luna. Even the "Goddess" of Christianity, the Virgin Mary, has some associations with the moon, since she is regarded as the Queen of Heaven with the moon under her feet (the Egyptian Goddess Isis was also considered such a heavenly queen). So, for Witches, the moon is special because it is a powerful symbol of the Goddess, and therefore of women.

Consider the phases of the moon. A new moon gradually waxes (grows larger) until the moon is full. But as soon as the moon is full, the waning (diminishing) process commences, until the moon cannot be seen in the night sky and is once again new. The three phases of waxing, full, and waning correspond to the three faces of the Goddess, and also correspond to the three ages in a girl's and woman's life.

✪ The waxing moon corresponds to the Maiden aspect of the Goddess, who in turn corresponds to a girl prior to the onset of puberty.

✪ The full moon corresponds to the Mother aspect of the Goddess, corresponding also to the years in which a woman menstruates and is at least potentially a mother.

✪ Finally, the waning moon corresponds to the Crone aspect of the Goddess, comparable to the years in a woman's life that begin with menopause, a time of age but also of wisdom.

Instead of saying that Witches worship the moon, it may be more accurate to say they revere her as a powerful symbol of the feminine force in nature. Of course, Witches believe that all nature is sacred and worthy of our veneration. In that sense, the moon is just like the sun or the earth in being worthy of respect and devotion.

Why is Halloween so important to Witches?

If there is one day of the year linked with Witchcraft, it's Halloween. March 17 may belong to the Irish and November 11 to Veterans, but October 31 will be forever linked in the popular mind with cackling hags riding on broomsticks to their midnight rendezvous with their weird sisters.

Like so many other stereotypes involving Witchcraft, there is a kernel of truth beneath the inaccuracy. Witches don't fly on brooms or wear pointy hats, but they do revere Halloween (which Pagans prefer to call Samhain, a Gaelic word meaning "summer's end") as one of the eight holy days of the year.

In pre-industrial cultures, Samhain signified the time when harvest was drawing to a close and the people needed to prepare for the coming cold winter months. It was a time when farmers needed to carefully evaluate their livestock, and slaughter any animals not expected to survive the winter. So it became a time associated with death and endings. According to the cosmology of the ancient Celts, Samhain is an "in between" time, in between the light/summer half of the year and the dark/winter half. As such, it is a time when the mystic veil separating the physical universe from the other world (the Summerland) is thin enough that spirits were able to, if only for one night, traverse between the worlds. With the energies of death in the air and the possibility of spirits roaming freely, customs arose around Samhain to provide spiritual protection, such as the wearing of costumes and masks to protect the wearer from unfriendly spirits.

To the Celts, the new year began not at the beginning of spring, or the middle of winter, but at the end of summer. Thus, Samhain marked the passing of the old year and the coming of the new. Many Witches follow this tradition and consider Samhain to be a new year's celebration.

From honoring the passing of the harvest season, to remembering those who have died, to solemnly giving thanks to the animals that must be slaughtered to provide food for humankind, Samhain has a powerful, solemn meaning. Witches see this night as meaning far more than a chance for children to wear colorful costumes and gather candy bars from their friendly neighbors. To Witches, it is a time to ponder the mysteries of life and death, to remember loved ones who have passed to the other side, and perhaps even to establish psychic contact with them.

What other days qualify as Wiccan holy days?

Samhain is probably the most important of the eight Pagan holidays known as the Sabbats; but to people dedicated to Wicca or other Pagan paths, each of the holidays has its own importance and beauty. This list is based on the seasons in the northern hemisphere; in the southern hemisphere, the calendar is inverted, so that the Winter Solstice is in June and the Spring Equinox in September, and so forth.

- ✪ **Yule or the Winter Solstice (approximately December 21st):** The longest night of the year is a time to celebrate the rebirth of the sun. Witches gather on this night to call the sun back from its southward journey. It is a time for feasting, singing, merry-making, and the exchange of gifts.

- ✪ **Imbolc or Candlemas (February 2nd):** This holiday is particularly sacred to the Celtic Goddess Brigid, a Goddess of healing, poetry, milk, and fire. It marks the first hints of the coming of spring, and in ancient times would have been celebrated about the time that the pregnant ewes began lactating. In honor of the Goddess associated with this date, it is a time for gathering around a fire and sharing poetry and other creative efforts.

- ✪ **Ostara or the Spring Equinox (approximately March 21st):** Ostara was a Germanic Goddess of springtime and the dawn, so it's only natural that her sacred day would be this equinox. Symbols sacred to Ostara include eggs and rabbits. If all this seems familiar, that's because the Christian holiday of Easter takes its name from Ostara (also spelled Eostara or Eostre).

✪ **Beltane or May Day (May 1st):** As Samhain marks the end of summer and the coming of winter, Beltane marks the opposite transition. This festival celebrates fertility and the onset of a new year of planting crops and tending livestock. In ancient Ireland, the Druids would light two huge bonfires and drive the animals between them in a ritual of purification. Today's Witches still like to build a roaring fire on May Day; jumping over it is seen as lucky, especially for young couples desiring a baby.

✪ **Litha or the Summer Solstice (approximately June 21st):** The opposite of Yule, Litha marks a turning point, as the night reaches its shortest length and the day its longest. This is a time of year particularly well suited for marriages (or handfastings), a custom echoed in society at large with its love of June weddings.

✪ **Lughnasa or Lammas (August 1st):** Named after a Celtic God of many talents, Lughnasa originally was a festival somewhat like the Olympics, where games and athletic competitions would be held. It also marked the beginning of the harvest season, and would be celebrated with the baking of bread made from the first grain harvest.

✪ **Mabon or the Fall Equinox (approximately September 21st):** Like Ostara six months earlier, this date is a time when daylight and nighttime are equal. It marks the precarious balance between light and dark, with light giving way to dark as the movement toward the Winter Solstice continues.

✪ **Samhain or Halloween (October 31st):** The harvest is completed and summer comes to an end; and so the old year passes and a new one begins.

Whereas full and new moon rituals are seen as more day-to-day rituals, the celebrations of the eight Sabbats are regarded as the holy days of Wicca. Often, covens will join forces to celebrate each Sabbat together, forming a large gathering that can truly celebrate the holiday in style.

Why do Witches like to burn candles and incense and use essential oils?

To Witches, these items are more than just spiritual window-dressing. Each herb or scent or color has symbolic meaning that helps Pagans to focus their attention on the purpose of a ritual or a magical working. Lighting a candle is more than just a nice accent for a well-decorated house; it is giving energy (the flame) to a color and/or a scent that supports the spiritual intention of the Witch. So, Witches who are seeking spiritual assistance to manifest more money in their lives might light a green or a gold candle, while those seeking a passionate romance might light a bright red one. Most books on Witchcraft or magic include detailed tables of correspondences explaining the spiritual meaning of colors and fragrances; by working with objects in accordance with these correspondences, Witches can focus their minds and their wills on achieving their goals.

The other primary purpose for using candles and related items is in ritual. In this setting, the emphasis is not so much on achieving goals, but on showing reverence to the Goddess and the God. Thus, ritually burned candles and incense are often chosen because of fragrances or colors believed to be pleasing to the God and the Goddess.

What is an altar? Why is it important?

An altar is simply a focal point for spiritual activity. As a general rule, this focal point consists of a table carefully decorated with candles, statues, and symbols of nature and the elements. Paganism is not the only spiritual tradition that uses altars. They are found in Catholic, Orthodox, and some Protestant Christian churches. But Wiccans and other Pagans believe that altars belong not only in church, but in people's homes. Thus, many Pagans have one or more altars set up where they live.

Although in ancient times altars were used for human and animal sacrifices, Wiccans never do anything on their altars that involves the shedding of blood.

A typical Wiccan altar might be a coffee table, covered with a lovely cloth. At the center of the table is two candles, signifying the Goddess and the God. Next to the Goddess' candle is a statue of a Goddess from world myth, with a similar God statue next to the God candle. Surrounding these items are four symbols of the elements of nature: an incense burner in the east symbolizing air, a red candle in the south symbolizing fire, a chalice filled with rainwater in the west symbolizing water, and a pentacle or a bowl of salt in the north symbolizing earth.

Also on the altar might be supplies for use in magic and rituals, such as candles, incense, oils, or herbs. Any food used during the ritual would be placed on the altar as well. Any tools used, such as an athame, would also be kept on the altar.

Altars are treated with respect. Non-spiritual items (such as ashtrays or coffee cups) should never be placed on an altar. It is considered disrespectful to place a foreign item on a Wiccan altar without the express permission of the altar's owner. It is also considered improper to touch a Pagan's altar or items on the altar without that person's permission.

Why is the altar important? As mentioned above, it is a focal point for the Pagan's spiritual practice. Pagans pray and meditate before their altars, and engage in ritual or magical work in the presence of the altar. The altar may be thought of as the "mission control center" for a Pagan's spiritual life.

It is not necessary to have an altar in order to be a Pagan. However, most followers of the old ways find that setting up their own personal altar is a meaningful and valuable way to bring the energy of their spirituality into their own home.

What is a circle?

A circle is a ceremonial/ritual/worship space for Pagans. But unlike churches, mosques, and synagogues, it doesn't have to be in a building. In fact, most Pagans prefer to create their circles outdoors.

Also, a circle is not a permanent structure. Some Pagans create permanent outdoor settings for their circles, often inspired by the ancient stone circles of western Europe (like Stonehenge). Others might plant a circular grove of trees with a meadow in the center where rituals may take place. And the more indoorsy Pagans might set up a "temple room" where their altar and magical tools are kept, and where the circle can be created.

But the actual circle itself is not a permanent structure. Instead, it is a field of energy that is created through visualization at the beginning of a Pagan ritual. At the end of the ritual, it is ceremonially dismantled. The circle may be thought of as a psychically constructed forcefield built around the ritual space. It defines the space just like the four walls of a church defines the space where Christian rituals take place.

To Pagans, creating this magic circle is a process of creating a sacred space where, just for a time, the Pagans can perform their spiritual activities in a "world between the worlds"—in other words, in a special place that is halfway between the physical and spiritual realms.

Among other things, the energy field of the circle contains the magical energy that the Witch (or Witches) generate during the ritual.

Most Witches like the idea of not having a permanent church building. To Pagans, the entire universe is holy. Setting up an energetic circle for ritual work is like pitching a tent for a restful night under the stars: it keeps the Pagan(s) in it closer to the worlds of nature and spirits, even when it is indoors.

Part Six:

Magic and the Occult

The world of Witchcraft is the world of magic. Occult rituals and enchanting spells have had a powerful hold on the human imagination, probably for as long as there has been an imagination! Different theories exist as to what magic is, what role it should play in Wicca, and how reasonable or helpful it really is. It is not the purpose of this book to explain all the philosophy behind magic. But hopefully, by reading the questions in Part Six, you'll learn why intelligent, educated people believe in (or at least are open to) magic, and how psychic or mental ability plays a central role in magical practices.

Magic isn't for everybody (in fact, not even all Pagans practice magic). But for those who are interested in it, it can be an intelligent, meaningful tool for spiritual growth.

Is Witchcraft part of the occult? What is the occult?

The word *occult* literally means "hidden." It refers to a philosophical and spiritual tradition in Western society, a tradition that has preserved and passed down hidden knowledge and information regarding human potential, humankind's relationship to the spiritual realm, and the theory and practice of magic.

The occult has a long history. It includes centuries-old disciplines such as alchemy (the quest for transformation, both on physical and spiritual levels) and the qabalah (an explanation of the spiritual dynamics of creation, derived from Jewish mysticism). Occultists study a variety of wisdom traditions, including astrology, Egyptian religion, Celtic wisdom, and Eastern mysticism. Over the centuries, entire organizations have existed dedicated to the pursuit of hidden knowledge, with exotic names such as the Rosicrucian Order, the Order of the Golden Dawn, and the Theosophical Society. Even some relatively mainstream groups, like the Freemasons, have some ties to the quest for occult knowledge.

Occultism sometimes has an unsavory reputation, for two reasons. First, it is denounced by religious conservatives as being evil or Satanic. This, as we have seen, is hardly unique to occultism.

Occultism also has come under fire from the scientific community, which denounces this secretive quest for inner knowledge as irrational or superstitious. Occultists freely admit that much of their work involves areas that can never be measured or verified by the scientific method. But to occultists, knowledge regarding spiritual mysteries or inner human potential does not need to be verified in order to be valid or useful. Occultists do not see science and the occult as competitive, but rather as complementary disciplines that approach the search for knowledge from different positions.

Many people, both within and outside of the Wiccan community, see Wicca as an occult discipline. Others, however, see occultism as an intellectual tradition, while Witchcraft is a more down-to-earth practice of healing and folk medicine, which does not need the cumbersome theories of scholarly knowledge. So opinion is divided on how closely Witchcraft and the occult are related. Either way, however, it's important to remember that critics of the occult and critics of Wicca and Paganism are often one and the same, and tend to be motivated largely by their need to assert that their religious perspective is the "only true way."

Are Witches psychic?

For many people, one of the most exciting characteristics of Wicca and Witchcraft is an enthusiasm for psychic and intuitive development. Psychic ability involves the mind's power to access knowledge through ESP, or to communicate with spiritual beings, or to create changes in the physical world through spiritual or mental power alone. Many religious groups have a curious discomfort or even hostility toward the mysteries of the mind. Wicca, however, embraces the frontier of mind power with gusto. A person does not have to be a psychic, or interested in psychic development, to be a Witch. However, since Witches believe that psychic ability is a perfectly useful and valid skill, many Pagans do pursue the development of their intuitive side.

Why is there so much resistance to psychic and intuitive development? Probably for a number of reasons. Because of the predominance of scientific rationalism in our society, some people see psychic inquiry as irrational. An entire industry of debunkers exist, writing books and publishing articles in magazines dedicated to exposing psychics and mediums as frauds. Often these people's gripe boils down to one essential criticism: psychic phenomena can't be measured using the scientific method. But to Witches, this doesn't make psychic phenomena invalid, it merely places psychic research outside the boundaries of traditional science.

Some religious groups also distrust the psychic realm, but for a different reason. They acknowledge the existence of psychic phenomena, but they claim it is evil, tricks of the devil used to lure unsuspecting souls away from the Lord. This is based on a few passages in the Bible that criticize mediumship (the ability to converse with spirits) or fortune-telling. Indeed, devout Christians may therefore decide they cannot in good conscience pursue psychic development. But Witches believe the Bible's anti-psychic stance is based on outdated principles. It's important to remember that the Bible also condemns divorce, the charging of interest, runaway materialism, and birth control. Nearly all Christians have learned to be flexible in their interpretation of such strict Biblical injunctions. In a similar way, Pagans believe modern people need to be flexible in regard to the legitimate pursuit of psychic ability.

Witches do not see psychic power as evidence that some people are more spiritually advanced than others. Psychic power is like athletic or artistic ability: everybody has it, but some are more talented than others. The point behind psychic or intuitive ability is to use the powers of our mind to help ourselves and others to live happier, healthier, more fulfilled lives.

What is magic, and why do Witches do it?

Magic is related to power. To possess magical ability means to possess spiritual power. Power, of course, is simply the energy to create change. So magic involves the ability to use spiritual means to enact change—change that may occur on a physical, mental, or spiritual level.

In the popular mind, magic appears to entail breaking the normal laws of physics. Causing physical objects to appear or disappear, or instantaneously change location, or suddenly change from one form to another: these are the popular images of magic. To actual practitioners of magic, however, the changes wrought by magic are much more subtle. Magic can mean changing a person's beliefs or thoughts, and as those mental changes occur, physical changes naturally follow. A person who believes he or she is attractive, for example, is more likely to enjoy success in love and romance. A popular business slogan proclaims, "What you believe, you can achieve." This is the very essence of magic.

Magic is not so much about breaking the laws of physics as it involves bending or shaping them. Magic begins with a basic principle of modern physics: that human consciousness interacting with the environment actually has an impact on the environment. Magic is the disciplined effort to consciously direct such impact and the changes that result.

The critics of magic are largely the same as the critics of occultism and psychic research. After all, the quest for magic has long been a central part of occult research, and psychic power is the basic raw material of all magic. Those who dismiss magic as irrational are locked within an outdated view of science, while those who insist it is evil tell us more about their dogmatic beliefs than about the merits (or lack thereof) of magic.

Why do Witches do magic? To Witches, magic is part of nature. It doesn't involve supernatural forces, but rather involves harnessing natural energies that science has not yet figured out a way to measure. Witches consider magic a part of nature, and nature is the sacred center of Pagan spirituality. It is only natural that Witches would want to apply magical power to their own lives.

Some people object to magic because it seems selfish or arrogant; all about "getting my own way," which could possibly occur at the expense of others. Indeed, many books published on the subject present it precisely as a tool for wish fulfillment. Most Pagans find this a limiting and spiritually questionable approach to magic. Magic is subject to the Wiccan Rede, which means any magic that harms another (even unintentionally) is prohibited. Most Witches find magic is best used as a tool for personal development or for healing work. There's no turning boyfriends into toads or bosses into jackrabbits. Instead, magic involves taking responsibility for self-improvement.

What do Witches mean when they talk about "energy"?

When Witches talk about magic, one word that appears again and again in their vocabulary is *energy*. "The energy of last night's circle was wonderful!" "I don't like my new boss. He has awful energy." "When you go to Stonehenge, you can barely feel the energy of the place now that it's turned into a tourist attraction." What do Witches mean when they talk about energy in this manner?

Perhaps the easiest way to answer this question is to turn to the East. Chinese and Japanese philosophy speaks of a fundamental life-force energy known as chi, qi, or ki, which animates all things and exists even within inanimate objects. Chi is essentially the energy of existence. Many eastern spiritual disciplines involve learning how to manage or direct the flow of chi. From Tai Chi to Qigong to Reiki, various physical and spiritual therapies from the East include the word chi (or its variants) in their name. Even the Chinese art of decoration and placement, Feng Shui, involves using architecture, interior design, and landscaping to facilitate the best possible flow of chi in the environment.

When chi flows properly, it brings vitality and health. When it is blocked, it can lead to misfortune or illness. Chi flows through the human body along lines known as meridians, and animates wheels of energy known as chakras. According to principles of Eastern medicine, when the chakras are open and the chi is flowing smoothly, the body is much more capable of attaining and maintaining wellness.

The energy of magic is basically the energy of chi. It is the energy of the Divine that is manifest in the physical universe. It is a sacred energy present in all things, constantly flowing and constantly changing. One of the central goals of magic is learning how to feel, manage, and direct the flow of this life-essence. Like all energy, magical energy is the fuel necessary to manifest changes in life. Magic is the use of spiritual symbols, mental affirmations, and ritual acts to help facilitate the flow of energy, thereby encouraging positive changes to occur in the world.

When Pagans talk about good or bad energy, often they are referring to an intuitive sense of how well (or poorly) chi is present in a person, place, or situation. A person with good energy is simply one whose chi is robust and dynamic, or calm and centered. A person with bad energy is someone whose chi seems blocked or frazzled. Similar distinctions can be made for the energy of a group, place, object, or event.

What is a Cone of Power? What is it used for?

One of the most common of magical practices involves a process called *raising a Cone of Power*. It's also called raising energy, raising a cone, or simply "a cone."

Many Pagans believe that energy such as chi is the fuel necessary to make magic happen. When energy is raised and dynamically present in a situation, it is easier for a Witch to work magic to make a positive impact in the world. Thus, Witches seek to raise energy as a core part of their magical work.

Whether a Witch is working as a solitary or part of a group, raising a cone involves exercises that generate the energy, and then a psychic (visualized) process of directing the energy toward its desired goal. It's called a cone because the energy is raised in a circular, spiral motion, that as it rises becomes tighter and tighter like a cone until it reaches a point where it can be psychically directed by the Witch to its goal.

How is the energy generated? Through chanting, drumming, visualizing, dancing, or other focused, energetic actions. While raising the energy, the Witch(es) visualize the purpose or intention for which the energy is being raised. When ready, the Witch (or in the case of a group, the High Priestess or Priest) releases the energy toward its goal.

Many Witches use cones for healing work, and so the purpose is to gather healing energy for the benefit of someone who is sick or convalescing. Cones can also be raised for general purposes (such as for environmental conservation or world peace), and even for political goals (such as supporting religious freedom or pro-environment legislation).

Raising a cone of power is generally considered to be an advanced magical skill, and most covens only entrust their elders or High Priest and Priestess with raising and directing the energy. Because the energy is seen as quite powerful, it is important for the Witch or Witches raising the cone to direct it only to positive, healing ends.

If a Witch has magic power, what's to prevent him or her from using it for bad purposes?

Power has a bad reputation. "Power corrupts, and absolute power corrupts absolutely," or so the saying goes. If magic is spiritual power, wouldn't it be a corrupting influence, and wouldn't those who wield it fall prey to its malevolent influence sooner or later?

Admittedly, the potential exists to abuse power—any kind of power. From Napoleon to Hitler to Osama Bin Laden, the world is full of tyrants and villains who have misused the power available to them. This, right away, is a clue to the truth about power.

Whether we like it or not, there really are people in the world who both have power and abuse it. And if no one ever stood up to them, we would all be their slaves.

Which leads us to the second truth about power: for every person who has ever misused power, sooner or later someone stepped up to the plate to stop them. Wellington stopped Napoleon; Churchill and Roosevelt stopped Hitler. Even Osama Bin Laden's evil transformed George W. Bush from a floundering U.S. President with no clear mandate into a world leader.

Power, like money, is neither good nor evil. Some people do abuse it, but others use it effectively and in service of the greater good. Witches approach power from this perspective. It deserves our respect, for it is a dangerous tool. Yet like any dangerous tool, it can be effective in the right hands.

Thus, the power of magic ought to be wielded by those with a commitment to service, healing, freedom, love, and nonharm (precisely the values of Wicca).

Let's keep this issue in perspective. Only in Hollywood do Witches have the ability to wield *supernatural* power. Real-life Pagans don't have access to special effects. Real Witches use magical power in simple and humble ways, because for them it manifests only in simple and humble ways. So if a Witch "goes bad," the main person he will hurt is himself. Psychologists who have studied magic theorize that the only thing that makes a curse work is if the victim believes in the curse. The curse in itself has no power. A Witch doing harmful magic won't hurt anyone, except for the spiritual toll it will take on himself.

Still, what is to keep a Witch from using magic for harmful purposes? The Wiccan Rede and the Threefold Law are the primary safeguards. Witches realize that there's so much freedom apart from harming others that there is no reason to even think about using magic in harmful ways. Furthermore, the Threefold Law promises blessings to those who use their energy in positive ways, but punishment to those who use magic to harm others. Given these odds, who in their right mind would use magic in any but positive ways?

Of course, I cannot guarantee that there's no such thing as a person involved in Witchcraft purely for selfish, unloving reasons. But there are similar problem individuals in any religion or any organization. For most Pagans and Wiccans, the clear ethical demands of the Rede and the Threefold Law are all that is necessary to keep magic oriented exclusively toward positive goals.

If Witches are such powerful magicians, why haven't they all won the lottery?

Many people seem to believe that magic should be the ticket to immediate wealth, courtesy of the lottery or some other gambling opportunity. This idea suggests that magic should automatically convey some sort of supernatural ability to guess the right numbers, or pick the winning horse, or whatever.

It's not because Witches don't like to gamble. Gambling in moderation is not considered a harmful activity, so Witches are free to indulge in it if they wish. The reason Witches don't clean up the lottery is because *magic doesn't work that way.*

Winning the lottery or guessing the winner of the Kentucky Derby would involve a supernatural level of psychic ability. Maybe somebody with that power exists somewhere, but if they do, they're a rare case indeed. Every New Age bookstore in the country has one or more professional psychics who have gifted intuitive ability, but they haven't racked up on the lottery, either.

Remember, magic and psychic skill are not what Hollywood make them out to be. The people who believe in the Hollywood idea of magic are fooling themselves. Witches and Pagans who devote years of study to the old religion come to understand that magic is very subtle indeed; it is a subtle energy used to create gentle but lasting positive changes in life. This is indeed powerful, but hardly dramatic or glamorous. And certainly not guaranteed to pick the winning numbers.

Some people might see this as evidence that magic (and therefore, Witchcraft) is fraudulent. But this comes out of a misunderstanding of magic. It would be like saying that cars are useless forms of transportation because they can't fly. Sure, magic is no ticket to supernatural power. But it still is a useful tool for personal transformation and for the focussing of healing energies. When we approach magic on its own terms, we can acknowledge its genuine, yet humble power.

Do Witches believe in astrology or Tarot?

Many Witches are avid students of divination, a branch of the occult that includes astrology, Tarot, the I Ching, numerology, palm reading, the runes, and other tools. The tools of divination are designed to provide answers and guidance for those who seek spiritual solutions to their problems. Some Witches and Pagans develop their skills in one or more of these tools to the point that they can make a living as a professional astrologer, numerologist, or Tarot reader.

The use of divination is not mandatory among Pagans, but just as magic is popular among Wiccans, so is divination. It seems to be almost a universal human impulse to seek divine guidance to help steer through the confusing or uncertain areas in life. But divination, like other magical or occult disciplines, is often misunderstood. Many people see it as little more than fortune-telling. Indeed, many people use astrology and Tarot in precisely this manner. While few Witches would say it's wrong to use divination as a tool for fortune-telling, many would say that this is a limiting use of these tools. At its best, divination is a process of exploring spiritual guidance through the use of symbolism. From astrology to numerology to the symbols in a Tarot deck or a set of runestones, all divination tools involve using symbols to find meaning and guidance in life. Such symbolism can be applied in very practical ways, as in asking a fortuneteller a question about the future. But when such symbolism is used as a tool for developing spiritual insight into the mysteries of life, then it can truly be a force for personal transformation. Most Pagans would say such inner transformation is the true purpose of divination.

Divination has its scientific critics who say it is irrational, or its religious conservative critics who say it is wicked. These critics miss the point. Divination is not meant to replace free will or personal responsibility. It is meant to provide a set of symbols that can be interpreted in a way to help people find spiritual meaning in their lives. Divination does not tell a person what will happen (or what to do), but enables the person to find the inner strength to take responsibility for life in a positive way. Used in this manner, divination tools become a powerful resource for a person's ongoing spiritual development. It is in this sense that most Witches find such tools to be useful and fascinating.

Do Witches believe in spirits, such as angels or fairies?

Another common element in magic and the occult is the belief in, and interaction with, spirit beings—entities who have no physical bodies, but who can communicate with human beings through dreams, imagination, intuition, and ESP. These beings could include angels, departed loved ones, fairies (nature spirits), Gods and Goddesses from world mythology, and maybe even extraterrestrials! The occult/magical/psychic world accepts the existence of spirit beings as a matter of course. Among people with no religious beliefs, such an idea may seem unusual; even religious people may have a hard time accepting the existence of spirits (although most religious people are comfortable with the concept of angels).

As a general rule, Witches and Pagans follow in the tradition of spiritually-minded people from the earliest shamans up to the most modern psychic researchers in accepting the existence, on at least some level, of the spirit world. Some Pagans may be rather skeptical, and say that spirits exist only in our imagination. Others take a more literalist view, and accept the idea that spirits really do exist "out there." There is no one correct *theory* of the existence spirits. But in *practice*, most Pagans are willing to at least go with the hypothesis that spirits do exist on some level and can interact with humans.

Part Seven:

Witchcraft, Christianity, and Other Religions

Paganism is as different a religion from Christianity as is Buddhism or Hinduism. Some people may be uncomfortable with this, if they are not comfortable with religious diversity in general. But today's world is a world where people of many different religions are learning to live in the same community with each other and get along. Wicca and other forms of Paganism are taking their place as valid religious paths, different from (but no better or worse than), any other religion. This section explores some of the issues related to understanding Wicca as one of many religious paths.

Some of the questions in this section explain how Wiccans feel about Christianity, and may seem critical or challenging to Christians. Please read such information with an open mind. Wiccans do not attack Christianity (or any other religion) gratuitously, but they do believe that honest criticism should be expressed. If you are a Christian, hopefully the perspectives presented here will help you to understand the differences between these religions, without meaning to attack or blame any spiritual path.

Witches call their religion "the old religion," implying that Wicca is one of, if not the, oldest religions on Earth. Is this true?

Religious groups appeal to the past as a way of justifying their spiritual teachings or claims. Every time there has been a reformation within Christianity, the leaders of the new movement argue that their brand of religion is more authentically in line with what the earliest disciples believed. In a similar way, the earliest proponents of modern Witchcraft argued for Wicca's merits by pointing out that the craft is a far older religion than Christianity or the other monotheistic faiths. To support this claim, Wiccans pointed to the evidence of ancient Goddess worship in cultures around the world as evidence of how old Goddess spirituality may be.

Certainly, modern Paganism seeks to revive ancient forms of spirituality and make them relevant and meaningful in our day. But it would be a mistake to view Wicca or any other form of modern Paganism as a religion that has existed in an unbroken tradition for thousands of years. Yes, there are some Witches and other Pagans who will say as much, but there is no evidence to warrant such a claim.

The issue here lies in the difference between religion as an organization, and religion as a tradition of spirituality. As an *organization,* Wicca and other forms of modern Paganism are all very young, dating back to the early to mid-20th century. But as a *spiritual tradition,* it is based on some of the most ancient spiritual practices, including shamanism, Goddess worship, and nature-based ritual.

We know the ancients revered the Goddess because of abundant archaeological evidence of figures and carvings of the Divine Feminine, as a Goddess of fertility and abundance. Meanwhile, research into Shamanism has suggested that it may well be the world's oldest spiritual path. Shamanism is the spiritual/magical healing practices of medicine men and women from tribal cultures. The shaman develops spiritual skills to find blessings and healing energies in the world of the spirits, and bring such positive energy back to his tribe. In many ways, Wicca is a modern urban expression of this most ancient of spiritual practices.

We know the ancients honored nature in their rituals and spiritual practices through the evidence of archaeological sites such as Stonehenge in England and Newgrange in Ireland, which are oriented toward the sun's movement through the sky over the course of the year. These sites reveal that ancient humankind had advanced astrological and engineering abilities, and relied on the natural world to provide a framework for tribal ritual and burial customs.

By calling Wicca the old religion, Witches do not mean to suggest that their way is any better or more authentic than other spiritual paths. It is simply a way of honoring the fact that this relatively new religion is based on some truly ancient practices.

What are the differences between Witchcraft and Satanism?

Witchcraft and Satanism are two entirely different spiritual traditions. There do exist Satanists who call themselves Witches, but this is a misuse of the word Witch.

Satanism is a parody of Christianity. All of the symbolism and rituals of Satanism are based on Christian rituals and symbols. In fact, the beliefs of Satanism are based on Christianity. Satanists take Christian beliefs and invert them. Satanism is Christianity turned upside down and inside out.

Incidentally, Satanism is not as big a problem as some people (mostly fundamentalist Christians) make it out to be. Yes, it does exist. There are plenty of Satanic Websites on the Internet, and there have been a few "celebrity Satanists" over the years, the best known being Anton LaVey. Satanists believe that Christianity is a weak and hypocritical religion, and they find meaning in Satan as a symbol of power and self-indulgence.

Satanism has nothing to do with Goddess worship. Nor is Satanism devoted to loving and protecting nature. Satanists are basically people who don't like Christian morality and who use inverted Christian symbols to express their dislike of Christianity. In other words, Satanism is a system based on hate—the hatred of Christianity and of Christian morals.

Wicca, Paganism, and authentic (Pagan) Witchcraft are not based on hatred, but on love. They do not make fun of Christian symbols and rituals, but are based on ancient Pagan symbols and rituals. Paganism, Wicca, and Witchcraft are moral and ethical religious/spiritual beliefs centered on worshipping the Goddess and loving and caring for the natural world.

To summarize:

Satanists	Witches, Wiccans, and Pagans
Worship Satan (the Christian devil).	Do not worship Satan. Few Witches believe Satan even exists.
Make fun of Christianity.	Regard Christianity as one of many valid religions.
Defile Christian symbols in their rituals.	Do not use any Christian symbols in rituals.
Do not worship the Goddess.	Worship the Goddess.
Have no policy in regard to the environment.	Believe strongly in caring for the environment.
Believe in no morality except for self-indulgence.	Believe it is wrong to harm others.
Tend to be contemptuous of those whose beliefs are different from their own.	Tend to be accepting and tolerant of those whose beliefs differ from their own.

If the person you love calls himself or herself a Witch, but is really more interested in Satanism than Goddess worship, then this book is not much help. But it's important for you to know that Satanism and Paganism/Wicca are two entirely different things.

What do Witches think about Christianity?

Witches consider Christianity to be a different religion from their own. Most Witches believe that there is no such thing as only one correct religion. To Witches, Christianity is one of several religions available to the spiritual seeker. In addition to Christianity, there is Judaism, Islam, Hinduism, Buddhism, Taoism, Confucianism, Native American Religions, Shinto, Sikhism, and of course, Shamanism, Wicca, and other forms of Paganism. Certainly there are many other smaller religions as well. Plus, nearly all of the major religions can be subdivided into many different sects, denominations, or traditions. There are so many different religious possibilities in the world that Witches think it is absurd to claim that any one religion is the only true way.

Just because Witches do not consider themselves to be Christians and disagree with the Christian claim of absolute truth does not mean that Witches hate Christianity. Most Witches simply see Christianity as another religion. Whether a person is a Christian or a Witch is no more momentous than if a person is a Democrat or a Republican. Sure, a Democrat may think the Republican is misguided in his or her views (and vice versa), but everyone accepts that in a democracy there will be differences of opinions and each person is entitled to their viewpoint. To Witches, religious differences are no more problematic than political differences.

Witches believe that some forms of Christianity are abusive or controlling, and that people who have been members of these ultra-strict forms of Christianity have a right to be angry about the abuse they received. But this is anger at religious abuse, which is different from hatred of the religion itself. Even the Witches who have been victims of religious abuse at the hands of Christians would say that Christianity is just as valid a spiritual option as any other religion.

Here are some of the more common criticisms that Witches have of Christianity:

- ✪ Christians can be intolerant ("My religion is the only true way") and can be pushy in trying to get non-Christians to convert.

- ✪ Christianity is sexist—it doesn't worship the Goddess and some branches of Christianity (such as Mormonism or Roman Catholicism) won't allow women to become ministers.

- ✪ Christianity is too conservative in its moral positions especially in regard to human sexuality between consenting adults (such as gay and lesbian people).

- ✪ Christianity does not do enough as a religion to protect the environment.

- ✪ The Christian Bible says that God will send most people to hell. Many Witches believe this is a scare tactic used to frighten people and is a blasphemy against Divine Love (which would never be so wasteful with its creation).

- ✪ Christians are hypocritical: they condemn Witches and other non-Christians for having liberal views of sexual morality, but then they don't live up to their own Biblical standards on such matters as taking care of the poor.

Not all Witches would be worried about these things, and most Witches understand that some Christians are better than others at taking care of the environment or tolerating religious diversity (just like some Witches are better than others at these same issues). But still, so many Christians tend to express religious intolerance or seem unconcerned about feminism or the environment that Witches tend to regard the entire religion as flawed in these ways.

But remember, just because Witches have criticisms of Christianity doesn't mean that Witches believe Christianity is bad or evil. Witches believe that the freedom of the Wiccan Rede applies to all people, not just Witches. Thus, anyone is free to be a Christian, as long as they don't cause harm through their beliefs.

Do Witches believe in Jesus? The Buddha? Etc.?

Witches do not believe that any one person is the ultimate expression of religious truth. So in that sense, they do not believe in Jesus the way Christians do, or in Buddha the way Buddhists do.

However, many Witches are avid students of world religion, and find that studying the teachings and ideas of great spiritual leaders is a valuable part of their own spirituality. They therefore tend to have great *respect* for Jesus, Buddha, Mohammed, Krishna, Moses, and other spiritual leaders, even if they stop short of *believing* in them.

Incidentally, in researching my book *Embracing Jesus and the Goddess*, I found that many of the Witches and Pagans that I interviewed had deep love and admiration for Jesus, even though they were not Christians. Many of these Wiccans had grown up in Christian families, and felt betrayed by a religion that they saw as unfaithful to the true message of Jesus. To many Witches, Jesus stands for principles such as love, forgiveness, personal relationship with God, and healing. But in many churches, Jesus appears as a stern figure who demands strict morality and total obedience, or else will send people to hell. Some people find that they love Jesus as he is portrayed in the Bible, but can't accept the Jesus who is proclaimed from Christian pulpits. It could even be argued that some Witches are actually trying to be *more* faithful to the spirit of Jesus' message by leaving Christianity and becoming Pagan!

Although in North America most Pagans come from families with Christian affiliation, it is true that some Pagans come from Jewish or other non-Christian backgrounds. All Pagans, whether they have Christian roots or not, tend to see Jesus as equal to great spiritual leaders of other traditions, and do not single out any one spiritual leader for particular devotion.

What do Witches think about the Bible? Do they have their own Bible?

Witches do not have a Bible of their own. In fact, Witches tend to be suspicious of the idea that a book can contain religious or spiritual truth. Granted, books can be helpful tools in communicating religious ideas or instruction. But to give a book absolute authority seems to be a way of placing a limitation on God and the Goddess.

Witches believe that spiritual authority is not revealed in a book, but is rather revealed in nature or in the heart and soul of each individual person. In other words, instead of reading a book that tells you about someone else's spiritual experience, Wiccans and Pagans opt for trusting in their own personal spiritual experience.

Witches don't have any strong feeling about the Bible, except that they decline to see it as an absolute authority. Pagans think that Christians who always try to prove a point by appealing to this or that verse from scripture are just arguing in circles.

If a passage in the Bible—or from any other sacred book of any religion—makes sense, then a Witch will accept it on its own terms. For example, the Bible teaches that it's wrong to kill. This makes good sense, because a society where murder is tolerated is no society at all. A Pagan will accept this teaching, not because it has some divine stamp of authority, but because it is reasonable and sensible. In other words, a Witch can accept religious teachings that do not conflict with the Witch's personal experience and understanding of nature.

But other verses in the Bible are not so easily accepted—for example, Revelations 20:15, which says that anyone whose name is not recorded in the Christian book of life will be thrown into a lake of fire (hell). This verse violates logic and reason, suggesting that the loving God whom Christians believe in will destroy most of his creation for no other reason than their religious affiliation. To Witches, statements such as these that violate common sense are evidence that the Bible, just like any other book ever written, has its share of flaws and imperfections. And because Witches and Wiccans don't believe the Bible has absolute authority, they are then free to disregard such teachings.

Witches do not single out the Bible for criticism. They try to use logic and reason when approaching any sacred writings from any religion. Thus, the Bible, the Koran, the Hindu Vedas, the Buddhist Dhammapada, or any other sacred text needs to be evaluated in the light of reason, experience, and common sense.

Can a person practice Christianity and Witchcraft, or Witchcraft and any other religion?

Witches have differing opinions on this question. Some Witches believe that Paganism is a complete and sufficient religion in itself, and therefore it would be a mistake to try to blend it with other religions. But many others think that interfaith spirituality is a perfectly valid path to pursue. Thus, there are Wiccans and Pagans who also incorporate elements of Christianity, Judaism, Hinduism, Buddhism, or other religions into their spiritual practice.

On the Internet there is a small but thriving community of "Goddess Christians" or "Christian Wiccans" who actively try to integrate Christianity and Paganism. There is also the concept of the "Jewitch" who actively tries to integrate Paganism and Judaism.

The Pagan community tends to be very tolerant of diversity, so even when Pagans experiment with other religions, there tends to be tolerance. But not all religions have such an open-minded culture. Many (if not most) Christians would say it is impossible to blend Christianity and Witchcraft. Certainly on the level of dogma, it would seem impossible, since Christianity has a number of dogmas (official teachings) that render it incompatible with Goddess spirituality, magic, or Paganism. But people who try to blend Pagan spirituality with other religions usually do so strictly on a personal spiritual level, de-emphasizing for themselves the differences in dogma. Instead they find creative ways to honor and worship both the Christian God and the Pagan Goddess.

Many Pagans believe that all Gods are one God, and all Goddesses are one Goddess. Within this concept, it would be perfectly valid for a Pagan to revere Jesus and Mary as their preferred images of the Divine Masculine and Divine Feminine. But Witches who did this would probably continue to revere other images of the Goddess and the God, such as Diana and Athena or Apollo and Pan.

Do Witches try to convert other people?

No. Witches and Pagans have no rules or principles about proselytizing. If anything, Pagans have a cultural bias *against* selling their spirituality to others. One of the reasons for the traditional cloak of secrecy surrounding Wicca is to make it harder to find—thereby ensuring that a person must want to be a Witch seriously enough that they will make the effort to locate a teacher or group. If a selection of Wiccan and

Pagan groups could be found just by looking up the topic in the yellow pages, there may be more people casually exploring nature spirituality who don't really feel drawn to it. According to this view, becoming a Witch is a serious matter, and only someone dedicated enough to pierce through the veil of secrecy deserves to follow the Pagan path. In other words, not only is Paganism opposed to proselytizing, but some Pagans actually want it to be difficult to become a Witch, to weed out those whose commitment is half-hearted!

Of course, many people who embrace the Pagan path love their newfound spirituality, and in the enthusiasm of their love, they may try to share it with family and friends. This can appear to be like a religious "sales pitch." But the difference between enthusiastic sharing of one's spirituality, and actively trying to convert others, is that the drive for conversion assumes that there is only one true spiritual path, and a person *must* convert in order to be accepted by God. Pagans have no such belief in the one true way, and so no matter how enthusiastic a Pagan may be in sharing his or her spirituality with family and friends, there is always an understanding that it's okay for others to say no.

Ever since Gerald Gardner published his first book on Witchcraft, it has been fashionable for Wiccans and other Pagans to write books about their spirituality. Many of these books, while not pressuring anyone to embrace Witchcraft, certainly do encourage their readers to follow the old religion. Such books have been wildly successful, with more and more authors and publishers bringing out introductory Pagan books all the time. Wiccan books are written in the spirit of sharing information, and of course they are used by people who take that information and thereby embark on the Pagan path. It is important to remember that there is no pressure in such situations. The author shares his or her knowledge freely, and the reader decides what to do with it. Indeed, the rapid growth of Paganism has more to do with how well it meets peoples' needs, than with any kind of conversion or proselytizing campaign.

My church teaches me that Witchcraft is wrong. Shouldn't I try to witness to Witches, in order to get them to repent?

This is certainly a difficult issue. Many Christians sincerely believe that every non-Christian is hopelessly doomed for the fires of hell, unless some Christian happens to preach the gospel to the lost soul in such a convincing way that he or she repents and embraces the way of Christ. Of course, there are also many Christians who believe in religious tolerance and diversity, and Pagans are generally much more comfortable with tolerant people, of any religious persuasion. But if you are troubled by your religion's message that Pagans and other non-Christians are doomed to hell unless you do something about it, hopefully the following ideas can help.

Christianity teaches that it is ultimately the Holy Spirit who compels people to become Christians. In other words, even if you are a Christian, it is not your job to save anyone. In fact, if you come across as so annoying to a person who might otherwise be interested in Christianity, annoying to the point that you push the person away, then you have actually undermined your religion, rather than promoting it!

To Pagans, the entire premise of convert-or-burn is absurd. Pagans believe in a loving Goddess. They say that such a Divine Mother would never condemn her children to eternal torment. To Pagans, the God of Christianity seems like a bully, aggressive, violent, and abusive. If you try to preach your religion in a pushy or combative way, Pagans think you are just embodying that same bullying and aggressive behavior. In other words, look into the mirror. If you really want to tell Pagans that the Christian religion is about love, make sure your behavior is always loving. Controlling, pushy, abusive, or combative behavior rarely comes across as loving.

Pagans trust that nature spirituality is the best religious path for them. They trust that there's no need to fear judgment or hell. If you want to communicate your fear about Pagans going to hell, you need to do it in a way that honors their trust. If you attack their trust, you will just come across as someone who is paranoid and fearful. Pagans don't want to trade in their joyful spirituality for one that is grounded in fear.

These are just a few of the reasons why Christians witnessing to Pagans rarely succeed in anything other than raising everybody's blood pressures. Pagans wish that Christians would stop trying to convert other people and start paying more attention to other parts of the Christian message (such as taking care of the poor, for example).

If you, as a Christian, are really worried that Pagans are going to hell, then go ahead and express your concerns to the Pagans in your life, but do so in a vulnerable, open-hearted way. In other words, instead of telling the Pagans why they are "wrong," simply share your fears and anxieties, talking about *what you feel* instead of *what you think about them*. Share why you believe so strongly in hell. Share why you believe a loving God would do such things. Share why you worry so much about Pagans, and why you believe your worry is a good thing. You may be surprised at how open and willing to talk many Pagans will be, if only you would approach them in humility and vulnerability, instead of with an agenda to save them. If you want Pagans to respect your religion and your spiritual practices, start by respecting theirs.

How can I tell if Witchcraft might be the right spiritual path for me?

It is not the purpose of this book to encourage you to become a Witch or some other form of Pagan. However, I realize that, in reading this book, some people may find that they are drawn to the Pagan path for themselves.

Basically, if you are interested in pursuing some form of Paganism for yourself, there are two things to do: read all you can, and interact with Pagans. As for the reading, begin with the books listed in questions 79 and 80. Don't just read one or two; get your hands on as many books as you can, and get to know the Pagan path as best you can. Usually, this process alone will help you to know whether or not your interest in Paganism is merely academic or represents a deep inner longing.

Reading books will help you to become knowledgeable about Pagan spirituality, but the ultimate test of whether you might want to become a Witch will lie in how you feel about meeting and getting to know people who are already on the Wiccan path. You can meet such people in relative safety and anonymity through the Internet by joining any of countless email lists, chatrooms, or bulletin boards that discuss Pagan and Wiccan themes. Just remember, online friendships are limited, so there may come a day when meeting one or more Pagans face to face is the next step. Presumably (because you are reading this book) you already know at least one Pagan person; that's the logical place to start. Another safe way to meet Pagans is through classes or lectures offered on nature spirituality in your community, usually at a New Age or metaphysical bookstore. In public forums you can meet people, get to know them, and see if your intuition encourages you to get to know them better.

The answer to this question is ultimately a very personal matter. Listen to your heart. Only you can decide. Remember, Witches do not believe that nature spirituality is the only way. You are free to become a Witch if you'd like, but no one in the Pagan world will think the worse of you if you decide it's not for you. Only you get to decide what's right for you.

Part Eight:

The Role of Paganism in Society

Nothing exists in a vacuum. Witches and other Pagans have to function in the same social and cultural setting as everyone else. This means dealing with the worlds of politics, money, income tax, and career. Unfortunately, it also means dealing with such issues as discrimination and prejudice.

This section addresses real-world issues related to Witchcraft and other forms of nature spirituality. From assessing the size of the Pagan community to appreciating the diversity of political beliefs among Pagans, the questions answered here can help you appreciate the world of Witchcraft in a down-to-earth way.

Is Witchcraft legitimate?

Witchcraft is protected by the U.S. Constitution. The freedom of religion that all Americans enjoy extends as well to Pagan religions, including Wicca. Any attempts made to curtail the rights of Witches must be seen as an attack on the Constitution, for a government that could take away the rights of Witches today, could take away the rights of Jews or Buddhists or Christians tomorrow.

As a religion, Witchcraft (and other forms of Paganism) is eligible for tax-exempt status as a nonprofit organization. But because Wicca originally began as a loose network of small groups that met in peoples' homes, there seemed no real need for groups to obtain official nonprofit status. To many old-school Witches, preserving their secrecy took precedence over having legal standing as an organization. This, however, is changing. Many Wiccan groups have grown beyond the size where they could function effectively in people's homes. Groups now put on festivals that attract hundreds of participants, or manage private nature conservancies, or publish magazines of interest to the larger community. More and more Pagan groups are handling significant amounts of money in their ministerial work, and more and more Pagan clergy are being called upon to perform official functions such as officiating at weddings and funerals or ministering to Pagans in hospitals or prisons.

Thus, beginning in the late 1970s and increasing ever since, many Pagan organizations have legally incorporated and sought (and received) tax-exempt status from the Internal

Revenue Service as religious nonprofit organizations. Like any other legal entity, these organizations have bylaws, boards of directors, and accounting procedures that enable them to comply with the relevant laws.

But incorporating and receiving tax-exempt status is not the only way in which Wiccan organizations have established their legitimacy. Many groups have a strong dedication to civic service as part of their Pagan ministry. Thus, more and more Pagan groups are engaging in conservation efforts; the cleaning up of forests, streams, or roadsides; prison ministry; and ministry to children (including religious education for youngsters). In all of these ways, Wiccan groups are increasingly establishing themselves as valuable spiritual resources in the communities they serve.

How many Witches are there today?

No one knows for sure. Unfortunately, a number of factors exist to make counting Pagans more difficult than taking a headcount of other religious groups. To begin with, many Witches and other Pagans believe in keeping their spirituality private. Such hidden Wiccans may not participate in voluntary censuses, and so can go unrecorded. Also, since so many Pagan groups are so small that they own no property and do no advertising or other public activity, they can go unnoticed by those who attempt to estimate the size of the community. For these reasons, any estimate is at best an educated guess.

An excellent essay found on the Internet, "How Many Wiccans Are There in the U.S.?" by B.A. Robinson (*www.religioustolerance.org/wic_nbr.htm*), explores the problems involved in estimating the Pagan population, and provides some guesstimates. Robinson suggests that there may be 750,000 Pagans in the United States and another 30,000 in Canada. That was in 1999. One factor that many observers agree on is that the Pagan community is growing rapidly.

Book sales can be one way to consider the size of the Pagan community. Some of the best selling Pagan books have sold over 300,000 copies. Given how many different Pagan books have been published over the years (not every Witch will own every book on the subject) and that many books will be used or read by more than one person, it is reasonable to assume that the Pagan community could be rapidly approaching the million-person mark. According to Robinson, Barnes & Noble's online bookstore estimated in 1999 that there are 10 million American consumers who buy Pagan books. Of course, there's no way to determine how many of those people buy such books because they are Pagan, or just because they're interested in the subject. But even if just 10 percent of those book buyers actually embraced the old religion as their own path, that would make for a million Pagans.

Even at 750,000, Paganism is on of the largest minority religions in North America, similar in population to Unitarian-Universalism, Buddhism, and Hinduism. Robinson also estimates that the Pagan community could be growing so rapidly that it is doubling in size every two to three years. If this is so, then Paganism could become one of the three largest religions in the United States by 2010. One thing seems certain: Paganism is here to stay.

Do Witches suffer from discrimination in our time?

Unfortunately, yes. Despite the constitutionally protected right guaranteeing freedom of religion, Pagans have experienced harassment, problems with child custody, employment discrimination, and even housing or leasing discrimination because of their religious affiliation. Witches who own retail establishments aimed at serving the Pagan community have been the targets of vandalism and harassment. Pagan groups have come under fire from local governments that have tried to prevent groups from meeting in private homes, even though in the same jurisdictions Christian groups can gather in private homes with impunity.

Several Websites on the Internet serve as watchdogs, keeping on eye on legal issues facing Witches and Pagans because of their religion. These include the Lady Liberty League (*www.circlesanctuary.org/liberty*) and the Witches' Voice (*www.witchvox.com*). Visit these Websites to learn about specific cases and current issues where first amendment rights have been violated.

Most Pagans and Witches feel quite strongly about problems of discrimination. Freedom of religion doesn't just apply to the major religions that everyone has heard about. Just because some people misunderstand Wicca and erroneously accuse Witches of evildoing does not give them the right to attack religious freedom. Some of Wicca's more prominent critics (such as Congressman Bob Barr [Georgia-R] who in 1999 spoke out against Wicca's presence on U.S. Military bases), argue that Wicca is not really a religion and therefore does not qualify for protection under The Constitution. But this in itself is a form of discrimination. It's like the old racist idea that African-Americans were not "really" human beings, and therefore deserved to be slaves.

More and more Pagans and Witches are speaking out against religious discrimination, not only for the Pagan community, but for all religious groups. Pagans who experience discrimination can turn to organizations like the Lady Liberty League for legal referrals or other assistance. Pagans believe that religious discrimination is just plain wrong, and many have therefore made the commitment to fight for the rights guaranteed by The Constitution.

What rights do Witches have at work? At school?

The same rights that anyone else has.

Many Christians carry Bibles with them wherever they go, and expect no one to harass them, tease them, or otherwise make an issue out of their religion. But Pagans have experienced discrimination just for having books on Witchcraft or related subjects in their possession.

Many Christians wear crosses on their rings or necklaces, and expect no harassment or discrimination for doing so. But Wiccan students have been harassed and sent home for wearing Pentacles at school.

Christians think nothing of talking about church, or quoting from the Bible, or making references to "God" or "the Lord" in their everyday conversation. But if Witches expressed elements of their religion in their everyday conversation, they could face social disapproval from others.

Pagans believe that in a society where freedom of religion is a basic right, schools and workplaces should be places where evangelism and proselytizing are not allowed. When members of a majority religion try to convert others, it can create an atmosphere of pressure that can interrupt productivity.

No Pagan wants to take away the rights of members of other faiths to practice their religion as they see fit in private. But Pagans want to enjoy the same public freedoms that anyone else enjoys, including the freedom to express one's faith in limited appropriate ways without fear of reprisal, and the freedom from attempts at conversion from the adherents of other faiths.

What do Witches believe about abortion? The death penalty? Gun control? Gay rights?

Most Pagans believe in freedom of personal conscience, and this extends to political views. There is no rule in the Wiccan world that says you must be a liberal, or conservative, or whatever. For this reason, different Pagans will hold different views about any controversial political issue. This is especially true of issues like the death penalty or foreign policy.

When it comes to social issues (such as abortion or gay rights), many Witches tend to believe strongly in personal freedom. Once again, personal conscience rules. Paganism is a spiritual path that stresses each person's unique connection with the Divine. Because of this, many Pagans resist the idea that government (or religion) has any business telling people how to behave, particularly in regard to sexuality. While it is appropriate for government to safeguard peoples' rights (which is why laws against rape or incest make sense), when it comes to consensual behavior, Pagans generally believe in personal choice over public policy.

So, in the examples of controversial issues mentioned in this question, Pagans might be divided over issues like the death penalty or gun control. But regarding issues such as gay rights or abortion, Pagans generally opt for the socially liberal position. For this reason, many Pagans tend to be either liberals or libertarians. But again, it's inaccurate to draw stereotypical conclusions.

Perhaps the two political arenas where Pagans tend to be most strongly identified include environmental policy and feminist concerns. Because of its Goddess orientation, Wicca and other forms of Paganism tend to be feminist-friendly; and because of the emphasis on reverence for nature, many Pagans take environmental concerns seriously.

What does the U.S. Military think about Witchcraft?

The United States Armed Forces have been generally quite positive in their dealings with Witchcraft and Paganism. Even though some Pagans are conscientious objectors to military service, many others believe it is an honor to serve in the armed forces. Furthermore, the warrior ethic of ancient cultures means that many Pagans consider it a particular honor to serve. Military Pagans take pride in serving their country, and so it is gratifying that the military has been positive in its treatment of Wiccans and other Pagans. Many bases have volunteer Pagan chaplains and active Pagan communities that provide religious fellowship, rituals, and classes for military personnel.

Here's an example of the positive status that Witchcraft has in the U.S. Military: In 1990, the U.S. Army published a guidebook for its chaplains in dealing with soldiers who practice a minority religion. This book includes a detailed, balanced, and fair description of Wicca and the unique spiritual needs of Wiccan and Pagan soldiers. The message is clear: in the army (as well as the other branches of the service), freedom of religion means that it's okay to be a Pagan.

Of course, not everyone agrees with the military's positive policy toward Wiccans. In 1999, U.S. Representative Bob Barr, a Republican from Georgia, made several public comments attacking Wicca's presence on military bases. Barr represented one of the most conservative districts in the country, and may have been taking a stand to please his constituents (although the Wiccans in his district were hardly pleased). Fortunately, Barr's voice represents a minority position, and most Americans understand that freedom of religion naturally extends to the armed forces.

For more information about Pagans in the military, visit the Pagan Military Network's Website at *www.milpagan.org*.

What social and political issues are important to most Witches?

Witches and other Pagans vary in their concern over different public issues. Pagans can be Democrat, Republican, or independent; conservative, moderate, or liberal. No one set of issues can be identified as being of special concern to Pagans. However, given the nature of Pagan spiritual beliefs, the following issues often are of concern to many members of the nature spirituality community:

- ✪ **Religious freedom issues,** especially protecting the rights of members of minority religions to practice their religion with the same level of freedom enjoyed by Christians.

- ✪ **Environmental issues,** particularly involving both short-term and long-term protection of the natural world, and efforts to clean up existing environmental problems.

    Pagans may differ in how they feel environmental policy ought to be implemented (libertarian Pagans, for example, tend to distrust government regulation, even when it is intended to support a clean environment), but generally they share a common belief that because nature is sacred, it is humanity's duty to preserve and protect her.

✪ **Social freedom issues,** especially in regard to gay and lesbian sexuality or other forms of sexual expression among consenting adults.

Many Pagans believe that the sexual values of society should be based on civil liberties and psychological norms, not on values derived from religion. Christianity tends to advocate a conservative view of sexuality, seeing it appropriate only within a heterosexual marriage. Pagans are much more tolerant of sexual diversity among consenting adults, although most Pagans would not necessarily be activists in this area unless they were fighting for policies that specifically pertained to them. For example, gay and lesbian Pagans are more likely to be involved in the fight for gay and lesbian rights.

✪ **Feminist concerns.**

As a Goddess-oriented religion, Wicca is practiced by women more than men, and tends to be popular in the feminist community. Thus, many Wiccans identify as feminist, and participate in political activism on behalf of women.

Remember, these are generalities; not all Pagans or Wiccans will share the same level of concern about any one issue.

Can gay and lesbian people be Witches?

Although I suppose individual covens could theoretically have rules prohibiting gays and lesbians from joining, I don't know of any covens that have such restrictions. On the contrary, the Pagan community tends to be highly accepting and supporting of gay, lesbian, bisexual, and transgendered persons. As noted above, most Pagans believe in freedom of personal conscience when it comes to expressing consensual adult sexuality.

The traditional forms of Wicca, with a male God and female Goddess joining together as lover and beloved, are steeped in heterosexual imagery. This is not meant to discriminate against gay and lesbians; the gender imagery in Wicca is meant to convey fertility more than just sexuality. Even so, some gay and lesbian Pagans have found greater comfort by creating new forms of Paganism that directly meet the needs of their communities. The Radical Faery tradition particularly serves gay men, while the Dianic Wiccan tradition particularly serves lesbians. However, a person does not necessarily have to be gay or lesbian in order to be a Radical Faery or a Dianic.

Many Pagans, whether straight or gay, believe that the Goddess and the God reside inside each individual person. Thus, sexuality is not about just uniting a male and a female, but rather begins with each person uniting within themselves their "inner God" and "inner Goddess." When a person has integrated both the feminine and masculine elements of their own soul, they are then more available to reach out in love to someone else, whether in a gay or a straight relationship.

Can a teenager become a Witch?

If teenagers become interested in Goddess and nature spirituality, they certainly can study it and learn all they can about it. Some covens even have classes specifically designed for teens. However, even if the teen's parents are not Pagan, covens typically require parental permission before agreeing to teach a minor.

Studying Witchcraft is one thing; actually becoming a Witch is something else. Many Pagan groups require candidates for initiation to be at least 18 years old, although that is not a universal rule. Strictly speaking, there is no spiritual reason why a teen cannot become a Witch; but practically speaking, many covens believe reaching the age of maturity as a prerequisite makes good sense.

Fortunately, with so many good books available, a teen interested in the craft can find plenty of literature and exercises to keep busy with personal study, until the day comes when he or she is old enough to pursue formal membership in a coven. For a list of books that are especially helpful for teens, please see question 79.

Part Nine:

Practical
Considerations

Assuming you've read the preceding sections of this book, by now you have a basic understanding of the Wiccan world. But you may still be wondering just what you need to do to quit having so many religious arguments with your teenager. Or you may be thinking you want to do more research on this subject. You might even be interested in attending a Wiccan ritual, but are shy for fear that you'll commit some sort of embarrassing faux pas.

These questions address such practical concerns. In this section you'll learn what to do (and what not to do) when relating to the Wiccans and Pagans in your world. You'll also learn where to go to take your studies further. Questions 73 and 79 will be of particular concern to parents, who may be trying to figure out ways to work out a teenager's interest in the old religion in a safe and responsible manner.

I'm a parent of a teenager interested in Witchcraft. Is there anything I should be worried about?

Like any parent with a teenage child, I understand the unique dilemma of wanting to give the child his or her freedom while also setting appropriate limits. Religion may be a particularly sensitive area. As adolescents grow up, it is essential that they learn to make their own decisions and act in accordance with their own conscience. Yet as parents, it is our job to recognize that we may not like or agree with all of our children's decisions. We need to find the right balance between giving them the freedom they deserve, and trusting our intuition and values as parents.

The essential issue here is the child's safety, both physical and spiritual. It has been the aim of this book to reassure parents that Wicca and Paganism are honorable and ethical systems that are spiritually safe. Physical safety, however, requires that your child associate with reputable and ethical people and organizations. Just as you want to have a sense that your child's friends are mature and responsible, you'll want a similar sense that any Pagans with whom your child interacts are mature and responsible people. If you are not yourself involved in Wicca or Paganism, then it makes sense for you to meet the leaders of any Wiccan/Pagan organization your child joins. Indeed, reputable Wiccan priests and priestesses will insist on written parental permission before they will allow minors to participate in their classes or rituals.

Some parents may require their children to wait until age 18 to participate in a Wiccan group. In the meantime, the child can always read books and learn all they can about nature spirituality on their own (see question 79 for recommended books for teens). This allows the child to pursue their interest, but sets a boundary that the parents feel is safe.

Other parents may allow their teens to become involved in a Wiccan group, but insist on participating alongside their children in any classes or rituals that their child attends. Indeed, I have known more than one adult who embraced the Pagan path because they were chaperoning their child's interest in the old religion, and developed an interest of their own.

As a parent, it is your right and responsibility to set limits that protect your child's safety. You can set those limits without violating your child's right to believe in accordance with his or her conscience.

One more area where parents of teens need to pay attention: if your child's interest in Witchcraft is primarily an interest in magic, that's worth exploring. Why is magic so important? Is your child just trying to compensate for feeling powerless in today's world? If so, it's important for your child to understand that Paganism is more than just casting spells, but is actually a spiritual and religious tradition as demanding as any other path. In other words, if your child is drawn to Wicca because it seems to be a quick fix to life's problems, he or she will likely be disappointed—and the problems will remain unsolved. You, as the parents, are responsible for helping your child develop enough self-confidence to face life's problems through their own initiative and efforts. Ultimately, that's where the real magic lies anyway. Wicca, as a spiritual path, can help a person willing to take responsibility for his or her own happiness. But Wicca can never make happiness appear like a rabbit being pulled out of a hat.

Can a person become a Witch just from reading a book?

As I explained in my book *The Well-Read Witch*, many people initiate their journey on the path toward Paganism by reading books on the subject. Hundreds of books are available on the subjects of Wicca, Paganism, magic, shamanism, ritual, and psychic development. Some books have ceremonies of self-dedication or self-initiation into Wicca. A person can read the book and follow the detailed step-by-step instructions on the ritual. However, among the elders and long-standing members of the Pagan community, opinion is divided over whether such a homegrown ceremony actually makes one a Witch. One Wiccan priestess explained to me that it is one thing to adhere to the beliefs and practices of a religion, but another thing altogether to be a member of that religion. Seen this way, a person can only truly be a Wiccan or a Pagan if he or she takes classes, joins a group, and receives membership through the group's ritual of initiation.

On the other hand, Wicca has a longstanding tradition of solitary practice. Solitaries are people who practice Witchcraft all by themselves. By virtue of the solitary nature of their spirituality, such a person would never be initiated into a coven or group. Does that mean that they are not really a

Pagan? No, solitaries are just as Pagan as are members of covens or other Wiccan groups. But they became a Pagan not by reading the right number of books, but by a decision they make in their heart. In other words, someone could read every book on Witchcraft ever published and still not be a Witch, or could have never read a single book, and yet still be a true Pagan within.

If someone you know is reading books on Witchcraft, that doesn't necessarily make him or her a Witch. But if their heart is embracing the old religion, that cannot be denied, even if they have never been through a formal ritual to make them a member of a Pagan organization.

For you, the person on the outside, this has an important ramification. Get to know what is important to that person's heart. Do they seek the love of God and the Goddess? Are they dedicated to healing the environment, or living a better, simpler life? Do they love nature, and want to learn from the wisdom of the natural world? A true Witch, by whatever name, would say yes to all of these.

What will the neighbors think? What do I tell people when someone I love is Wiccan?

If your spouse or child or other family member embraces Paganism, you may be concerned about a number of related issues. What will the neighbors think? What will other family members say? Will there be repercussions for you, for your Wiccan loved one, or both?

These are normal concerns. Because Wicca and Paganism continue to be so widely misunderstood, it's reasonable to assume that other people in your life may not be open to it. There are several ways to deal with this concern. Traditionally, Witches and Pagans practice discretion in their spiritual life. They don't reveal their spiritual path to others unnecessarily. Spirituality is a private matter, and it's often a subject best left undiscussed, whatever a person's religious preference might be. However, this is not always a practical strategy. If your family member wants to perform Wiccan rituals in your backyard, your neighbors might understandably be curious. Furthermore, if some people in your life are pushy with their religion, it might be important to let them know why your daughter chooses not to attend church.

You may choose to become an activist for religious tolerance, writing letters to your congressman or local newspapers speaking out against religious discrimination. Of course, such concerns do not involve Paganism and Wicca alone. Many religious minorities, from Muslims to Sikhs to Santerians to Hindus, experience religious-based discrimination in our society. You (or your loved one) can become involved in programs to fight religious intolerance without ever revealing your connection to Paganism. Again, discretion is a good common-sense strategy.

There's no right or wrong way to tell (or not tell) others about Paganism and Wicca. If you are uncomfortable with your family member practicing Paganism, let them know your feelings. Try to negotiate an agreement about being discreet and private in their spiritual practice, even if only temporarily. That will enable you to feel safer.

Finally, remember that increasing numbers of people are feeling drawn to Wicca and Paganism all the time. The very people whose good opinions you wish to maintain may be more sympathetic to nature spirituality than you realize. Recently a conservatively dressed casual acquaintance of ours came to our house, and noticed a copy of *The Complete Idiot's Guide to Paganism*. When she realized I was the author of the book, she enthusiastically shared with my wife her interest in the subject!

Is there anything I should know about the etiquette of Witchcraft?

Now that you know at least one Wiccan or Pagan, you might have the opportunity to meet more. You may meet friends of the Pagan(s) you know, or you might even be interested in attending a class or ritual sponsored by a local Pagan or Wiccan community. Even if you have no interest in becoming a Witch or a Pagan yourself, contact with people who practice nature spirituality may now become a part of your life.

How do you behave around a Pagan or a Witch? What are the do's and don'ts? Here's a quick rundown of the main points that will help you avoid faux pas when interacting with members of the old religion.

To begin with, normal common courtesy applies. Just as it is impolite to make light of anyone else's religious beliefs, be careful about making jokes or humorous comments about Paganism. Many Pagans have a great sense of humor, but others may be touchy about their spiritual path. Also, while it is okay to say that you are not a Pagan and to say what your religious path is, it is just plain impolite to argue about religion or to suggest that you consider their religion to be inferior to yours (and hopefully if you've read this far, you are not someone who considers your religion to be superior to others).

✪ Never reveal a person's involvement in Paganism and Witchcraft to others without the individual's prior consent.

✪ Do not touch/handle Pagan religious objects without permission to do so.

✪ Do not assume that everyone who practices nature spirituality likes to be called a Pagan, or a Witch, or a Wiccan. Often, only one of these labels will be considered proper.

✪ Among Pagans, or at rituals, it is proper to use a person's "magical" or religious name. In public, however, it is generally considered more proper to use their legal name.

✪ If a Pagan has a religious title, it is proper to use that title when addressing him or her. The most common religious titles are "Lord" for men and "Lady" for women. These do not have legal or political implications (as they do in Great Britain); their meaning among Pagans is strictly honorific. Thus, a male Pagan might be known as "Lord Merlin" and a female Pagan as "Lady Athena."

✪ If you attend a Pagan ritual but feel uncomfortable about participating in it, say so. Most groups will suggest that you to sit outside while the ritual it is going on.

✪ As a non-Wiccan, if you attend a Wiccan ritual, you may be expected to sit outside the ritual during portions of it; some rituals (like initiations) are strictly for group members only, and you will not be allowed to participate at all. Do not take it personally if you are excluded from all or part of a ritual; this is a common practice in the Pagan community.

✪ Try to observe the customs regarding proper attire at rituals (although most Pagan groups do make allowances for guests). If in doubt, ask.

✪ Even though you are a guest at a Pagan event, offer to help with setting or cleaning up. Many Pagan groups probably won't let a guest help. But offer anyway.

✪ Offer a gift at rituals or other Pagan events, such as food, beverages, or a monetary donation.

✪ Don't be afraid to ask questions, but it's best to do so before or after the actual ritual.

✪ Do not throw anything used in a ritual into the trash, and do not blow out candles (use a candle snuffer).

✪ Allow yourself to enjoy the spirit of the gathering. Remember, even if you don't feel like your beliefs are Pagan, you can still enjoy the beauty and simplicity of a Pagan ceremony.

What do I need to do in order to get along well with the Witch in my life?

You may be wondering, "How do I treat Pagans and Witches?" Unfortunately, Miss Manners hasn't yet put out a book on the correct etiquette for proper relations between Wiccans and non-Pagans. Sure, common sense applies, but when it comes to treating Pagans in ways that work for both you and them, the rules are not yet written.

Still, based on common sense and general principles of interfaith relationships that apply to any two religions, here are a set of guidelines for getting along with the Witch(es) in your life. Hopefully, these pointers will enable you to relate with Pagans in the most constructive way possible. See question 78 for a further list of don'ts to help you avoid some of the more obvious pitfalls in dealing with Pagans.

1. **Agree to disagree.** No, you don't have to see eye to eye on every issue. It's better to accept this up front.

2. **Keep the serenity prayer in mind.** One of the most famous prayers, applicable to any religion, is beautiful in its simplicity: "Grant me the serenity to accept what I cannot change, the courage to change what I can, and the wisdom to know the difference." How does this prayer apply to relating to Pagans? Well, you cannot change another person's religious or spiritual choice, but you can change your ability to accept their choice gracefully and respectfully.

3. **Actions speak louder than words.** Many people want to "save" others from Paganism or Witchcraft out of "love." The thinking goes like this: "Because I love you, I want you to repent from the wickedness you've fallen into." But because Pagans and Witches believe their spirituality is a good thing, any efforts to save them will just come across as controlling and irritating. If you really love someone, why argue with them about a difference in religious belief? Pause and consider how you can show your love through actions, rather than talk about it with words. Being a good listener, showing respect, accepting what you cannot change, showing kindness and thoughtfulness: these are the hallmarks of love. Showing love will make a real difference in the life of the Pagans you know, while merely talking about love can come across as false or hypocritical.

4. **Respect privacy.** It is considered a breach of etiquette to reveal to non-Pagans that someone you know is involved in Paganism. It's really nobody's business whether your child or next-door neighbor is a Witch. The one exception to this rule would be if you feel the need to discuss Witchcraft in a trusted, confidential setting (such as with your therapist or counselor). Even then, there's no point in dwelling on what someone else's spirituality is, even if that someone else is your own child. A counselor cannot get your child to change religions, but can help you to accept the situation in the best way possible.

5. **Be aware of your relationship with nature.** One of the best ways to relate gracefully to a Pagan or a Witch is to clean up your own act in regard to the natural world. Start recycling, use natural products, eat organic foods, and drive fuel-efficient automobiles. To you, such actions may simply be good common sense, but to a Pagan they are signs of reverence and respect.

6. **Acknowledge your lack of knowledge and/or your fears.** Even after reading this book, your knowledge of Paganism will still be limited. It's good to admit what you don't know. And related to this is being honest about feelings. Many people in our society, especially those who come from conservative religious backgrounds, have been taught to fear the occult or magic. If you find that merely the subject of Paganism triggers a strong emotional response in you, it is likely that deep down inside you find the subject threatening or unsettling. Being honest about this, if only with yourself, can take you a long way toward relating to Pagans constructively.

7. **Express your feelings in positive/constructive ways.** If Paganism makes you nervous, talk about it. If Paganism scares you or gives you the creeps, admit it. Only, own your feelings for yourself; don't project them onto another person. In other words, say, "When I think about Witchcraft, I feel nervous," not, "You doing this magic stuff really upsets me." Also, keep your focus on the positive. Instead of, "I hate it that you are a Witch," try, "I want to find a way to feel more comfortable about your spiritual choices."

8. **Listen. No means no.** If you have strong religious beliefs, you may find that the Witch or Pagan in your life isn't interested in talking about it. Do not take this personally. Pagans and Witches have had plenty of encounters with Christians (or others) telling them what they should believe or think. If a Pagan tells you they do not want to go to church with you, or pray with you, or talk about the Bible with you, respect their limits. If they ever reconsider, they'll let you know.

9. **Ask questions, but only when you really want to know the answer.** One of the best ways to interact with Pagans is to ask them questions about their path. After all, Pagans tend to be enthusiastic about spirituality, and so this enthusiasm can inspire an honest and intimate conversation. But don't do this unless you are sincerely interested in learning about the old religion. If you're just trying to pick a fight or discover holes in their logic, you'll end up alienating the person, instead of drawing them closer.

10. **Trust.** Trust the good intentions of the Witch in your life. He or she is not out to get you, to threaten you, or to hurt you. Also, give the benefit of the doubt. Like anyone else in our culture, Witches are innocent unless proven otherwise. When you approach Wiccans with an open and trusting mind, it is easier to simply relate to them as human beings.

11. **Look for common ground.** Okay, maybe your religious and spiritual beliefs are poles apart. But you may still have much in common with the Pagans

in your life. You may not share religion, but you still have similar values when it comes to hobbies, entertainment, politics, or work. Emphasize what unites you, not what separates you.

12. **See the Witch in your life as a teacher.** Even if you don't want to learn about Paganism, you still may have a thing or two to learn about diversity, or religious tolerance, or simply loving your child or friend or coworker for who they are, not for who you think they should be. Now matter how old you are or how educated you consider yourself to be, there are always new lessons in life. Approach the Witch in your life with this kind of humble openness, and you may be pleasantly surprised at the insights awaiting you.

13. **Keep your agreements.** This includes the agreements you've made with or in your own religion. Christianity, for example, enjoins its followers to be loving, forgiving, and kind, even toward their enemies. Of course, Wiccans and other Pagans are not your enemies! No matter what your opinion is of Paganism, if you treat Pagans with the kindness your religion expects you to show to others, then you've taken the most important step toward creating a positive relationship.

What should I *avoid* saying or doing when relating to the Witch in my life?

The answer to question 77 provided a set of guidelines you can follow to foster a positive relationship with your Wiccan or Pagan child, co-worker, or friend. But there are also a number of missteps you can make when relating to Witches. This chapter points out some of the more obvious pitfalls worth avoiding. While it's written mostly in terms of parents trying to relate positively to teens who have embraced the old religion, the principles can generally be applied to any situation where you as a non-Pagan are dealing with a Wiccan.

1. **Watch your tongue.** Okay, so maybe Witchcraft upsets you, scares you, makes you angry and furious, and you think your child is a fool for getting involved in such a spiritually questionable activity. What you think is what you think, and it's not my place to tell you you're wrong. But even if your feelings about Paganism and Wicca are this strong, think long and hard before unloading your opinions on the Witch in your life. All you'll do is push him or her away. In the long run, is that really what you want?

2. **Don't take it personally.** Having a teenager get into Witchcraft may seem like a personal attack on you. And yes, some people get into Paganism as a way of rebelling against their upbringing. But

if you insist on seeing Paganism only as an affront, you are robbing your Pagan child from finding the positive dimension of the old religion. Plus, tempting as it may be to paint this event as some horrible family tragedy, the truth is your child is acting no differently than thousands of other kids from all over the place. Kids always find a way to rebel against their parents. Remember, Paganism is an ethical, life-affirming religion. Having a Wiccan child is nothing more than a challenge to your beliefs—as opposed to a real tragedy, like having a child get involved in crime or drugs.

3. **Don't worry about the little things.** Okay, your child is wearing a huge silver pentacle, dressed all in black, and has dyed purple hair. You can work your blood pressure into dangerous levels over this, or you can maintain a sense of perspective. Remember, when you were a teenager, you dressed in ways that annoyed *your* parents. The fashion choices of Wiccan and Pagan teens constitute only a small part of the old religion. If you pick fights over your kid's jewelry, you'll lose the moral high ground you need to provide guidance to them where it really counts.

4. **If you must preach, preach love.** A common reaction to finding out that someone is a Witch or a Pagan is to talk about your own religious path. While there's nothing wrong in sharing your faith, be careful. If you talk about God in terms of wrath, judgment, sending people to hell, or anything along those lines, the Wiccan or Pagan in your life will quickly tune you out. Why? Because he or

she has heard it all before, and such images of judgment don't make sense to a person who believes in a loving, compassionate Goddess. So talk the language of love.

5. **Don't recycle arguments.** There's no point rehashing old conflicts. You and your child don't see eye to eye on going to church, or on reading the Bible, or on the use of Tarot cards. If you insist on rehearsing the same fight over and over again, you'll push them a bit farther away each time. If you don't see eye to eye on an issue, then agree to disagree. It will make life better for everyone.

6. **Don't be provoking.** Picking a fight is a waste of time and energy, and can put an additional layer of stress on an already strained relationship. Take this one a step further: not only should you avoid starting arguments, but also learn to defuse the situation if your Pagan child has a habit of trying to provoke you. You're an adult. Modelling mature behavior is an important way of parenting your child. It's worth it.

7. **Don't blame.** Even if you are convinced Paganism is a bad thing, avoid the temptation to look for someone to blame. It's no one's "fault" that Witchcraft has come into your life. Remember, hundreds of thousands of Americans and other people from around the world are embracing the old religion. You are far more likely to have a Witch in your life than you are likely to win the lottery; remember that the next time you buy a ticket! Also, be careful about blaming bad luck or misfortune on Witchcraft. Such superstitious thinking is linked

to old misconceptions. Remember, Wicca and Paganism have nothing to do with cursing or black magic. Christians, Jews, and other people experience bad luck in their lives. So do Pagans (and their relatives). Blaming bad luck on someone's involvement in the craft is plain irrational thinking.

8. **Don't tease or make fun.** A sense of humor is a good thing, and can help to ease the normal tensions of life. But it's one thing to make a silly pun or to gently poke fun at yourself; it's another thing altogether to make disparaging remarks about another person, or their religion. Just as sexist or racist jokes are considered offensive, so is humor aimed at religion, spirituality, or belief. If you find yourself wanting to make light of another person's beliefs, it may be time for a closer look at your own inner motives. Why is their belief so threatening to you that you feel compelled to make fun of it? Working on yourself would be a better use of your time than joking at someone else's expense.

9. **Don't be manipulative.** Saying things like, "How could you do this to me?" or, "If only I had taken you to church more when you were little!" solves nothing. Even if you honestly believe your Wiccan child is merely rebelling against his or her upbringing, making a big deal out of it solves nothing and is more likely to lead to further alienation. Making a show of blaming yourself or looking for some other "reason" why your child is Wiccan is similarly fruitless. If you don't like having a Witch in your family, own your feelings. Then be respectful and mature in how you deal with your Pagan

loved one. The more you exhibit mature adult behavior, the more likely your child will respond to the good example you've set and treat you in a similar way.

Many of these principles are based on the assumption that you don't like Witchcraft, or think it's a poor religious choice for your child to have made. As I've said, I cannot change your way of thinking. But I do need to point this out: if you learn to appreciate the beautiful and positive elements in the craft, you'll take a huge step toward relating to your Wiccan child in a constructive and harmonious way. You don't have to become a Witch to feel positively about Witchcraft. But if you do make the effort to see the old religion as an honorable and respectable religious option, I feel confident that your relations with Pagans will blossom.

What are some good Wiccan books for teenagers?

This question is intended to help parents and anyone else interested in or concerned about the spirituality of teenagers, to understand what kind of books are available, both written expressly for teens or written for a general audience but likely to be read by teens. Like anything else, Wiccan books for teenagers vary widely in quality. Hopefully, this guide will help parents and other concerned folks to know what's best, and be able to intelligently discuss these books with the teens in your life.

Increasing numbers of books are being published aimed specifically at teenagers or young adults with an interest in Paganism or Wicca. While this may be a worrisome trend (I know plenty of Wiccan elders who feel that teenagers shouldn't study the craft without parental permission, so it's worrisome not only to non-Witches), it's a reality.

Of course, many books on Wicca are not written specifically for teens, but are written in a simple and accessible style that intelligent teens will easily understand and enjoy. So even if publishers never put out another book aimed specifically at young people, that wouldn't eliminate the demand for Witchy books among adolescents.

If you are relating to a teen who is interested in Paganism, I heartily recommend you read some or all of these books yourself. The more knowledgeable you become on this topic, the more you will be able to truly relate to the adolescent who looks to you for guidance.

Scott Cunningham, *Wicca: A Guide for the Solitary Practitioner*. **Llewellyn Publications, 1989.**

This manual for do-it-yourself Witchcraft stresses trusting in your own intuition and honoring your own innate connection with the Goddess and the God. While not specifically written for teenagers, it is so basic that any intelligent teen will easily grasp its message.

Gerina Dunwich, *Exploring Spellcraft: How to Create and Cast Effective Spells*. **New Page Books, 2001.**

Another book written for adults but accessible to smart kids, *Exploring Spellcraft* gives an introduction to the many tools available for magical work, from astrology to Tarot to candles and other accessories.

Julie Tallard Johnson, *The Thundering Years: Rituals and Sacred Wisdom for Teens*. **Bindu Books, 2001.**

This isn't a Pagan book, but it's one of the best books on adolescent spirituality that I've seen, and many of the ideas presented in it are fully compatible with Pagan ways. A great book for adults and kids to share in supporting an adolescent's emerging spiritual maturity.

Lauren Manoy, *Where to Park Your Broomstick: A Teen's Guide to Witchcraft*. **Fireside Books, 2002.**

An ethically sound introduction to teen-specific Paganism, complete with a thoughtful introduction written just for parents.

Lilith McLelland, *Spellcraft: A Primer for the Young Magician*. **Eschaton Books, 1997.**

Written specifically for teenagers, this book provides a step-by-step introduction to magic and emphasizes ethics and responsibility as the foundation of the spiritual life.

Anthony Paige, *Rocking the Goddess: Campus Wicca for the Student Practitioner*. **Citadel Press, 2002.**

Most teens go to college, where they may have their first opportunity to interact wtih others interested in the Pagan path. This book explores the life of the "College Witch."

Jamie Wood, *The Teen Spell Book: Magick for Young Witches*. **Celestial Arts, 2001.**

After a brief introductory section, the bulk of this book consists of safe, simple spells on topics of concern to the typical teenager. The book stresses the importance of responsibility and maturity as prerequisites to any magical activity.

What are some good Wiccan books for adults?

Whether you are interested in learning more about Paganism and Wicca just for the sake of being well informed, or if you would like to explore this spiritual path for yourself, then the books mentioned in this section may be helpful for you. Remember, Pagans and Wiccans do not recruit converts, so you won't find a "hard sell" in any of these books. If this spirituality is for you, you won't need a book to tell you so. Conversely, if it's not for you, reading a book won't trigger a dramatic conversion. But whether or not you might have a personal stake on the old religion, I hope you'll take a closer look at some or all of these books. I believe education is one of the most important ways in which we can foster respect and compassion between people who have different religions or different beliefs (or, for that matter, different nationalities, political views, or ethnicities). Merely reading about a faith different from your own in an open-hearted manner is a way to take a stand for religious freedom and tolerance.

Margot Adler, *Drawing Down the Moon: Witches, Druids, Goddess-Worshippers, and Other Pagans in America Today*, Revised and Expanded Edition. Penguin/Arkana, 1997.

This book provides an overview of the entire Pagan movement, including Witchcraft, Druidry, and other traditions. It's a bit dated, having been written in the late 1970s, but easy to read and filled with useful information.

Phyllis Curott, *Book of Shadows: A Modern Woman's Journey Into the Wisdom of Witchcraft and the Magic of the Goddess*. **Broadway Books, 1998.**

Curott, a highly successful entertainment lawyer in Manhattan, tells her down-to-earth story of embracing the world of Wicca. This book provides an excellent insight into the value of Paganism for successful and intelligent people.

Gus Di Zerega, Ph.D., *Pagans & Christians: the Personal Spiritual Experience*. **Llewellyn Publications, 2001.**

Di Zerega explains the rationale behind nature spirituality, considers (and answers) Christian criticisms of Wicca, and details (in a non-attacking way) the Pagan criticisms of Christianity. He successfully makes a positive statement about nature religion without gratuitously slamming the way of Christ.

Janet and Stewart Farrar, *A Witches' Bible: The Complete Witches' Handbook*. **Phoenix Publishing, 1984.**

An elegant and articulate introduction to British traditional Witchcraft, written by two of the most respected Witches within the Pagan community. Includes detailed information on the sabbats (the Witches' holy days) and sample rituals.

Amber Laine Fisher, *Philosophy of Wicca*. **ECW Press, 2002.**

An ambitious and beautifully written overview of the theology and philosophy of nature spirituality. Emphasizing the mystical rather than the magical dimension of Wicca, this book works well for those who may not be interested in spellcasting but still would like to know the ways of this modern Goddess tradition.

Ronald Hutton, *The Triumph of the Moon: A History of Modern Pagan Witchcraft.* **Oxford University Press,1999.**

An essential book for understanding the origins of Wicca. Hutton, a British scholar, takes a critical but fair look at the various people, ideas, and organizations that contributed to the birth of modern Witchcraft, which he places at sometime during the 1930s or 1940s. Even though this book argues that Wicca is essentially a new religion, the Pagan community has largely accepted it. I believe it sets the standard for Wiccan history.

Carl McColman, *The Complete Idiot's Guide to Paganism.* **Alpha Books, 2002.**

Written in the popular "Idiots Guide" format, this book gives the absolute basics of Paganism in a simple and easy-to-understand format. It reveals how Wicca and Witchcraft are simply one part of a larger trend toward reverence for nature.

Carl McColman, *Embracing Jesus and the Goddess: A Radical Call for Spiritual Sanity.* **Fair Winds Press, 2001.**

Gus Di Zerega's book approaches the question of Christian-Pagan relations through theology and philosophy, while *Embracing Jesus and the Goddess* looks at the issue from a more spiritual perspective. This isn't for everyone: many people, both Christian and Wiccan, will insist that the two religions are fundamentally incompatible. But for those who would like to at least try to integrate the spiritualities of Jesus and the Goddess, this book provides a roadmap.

Carl McColman, *The Well-Read Witch: Essential Books for Your Magickal Library.* **New Page Books, 2002.**

A guide to books on Paganism and Wicca. Over 400 books on a wide variety of topics are reviewed in *The Well-Read Witch*.

It starts with books on Paganism and Witchcraft, ranging from introductory titles to books written for long-time practitioners. It also includes books on topics that would be of interest to the advanced Pagan: ranging from mysticism to magic, from herbalism to psychic healing, from meditation to mythology. To know the Pagan mind inside and out, read the books profiled in this guide.

Philip J. Rhodes, *Wicca Unveiled: The Complete Rituals of Modern Witchcraft*. The Speaking Tree Books, 2000.
This is a beautifully designed book that gives a comprehensive collection of Wiccan rituals in a clear and easy-to-follow format. Because there is so much diversity in Pagan spirituality, not all Pagans or Witches will perform rituals like the ones contained in this book. Still, as a glimpse into the world of craft ritual, this is as good an introduction as any.

Starhawk, *The Spiral Dance, A Rebirth of the Ancient Religion of the Great Goddess: Rituals, Invocations, Exercises, Magic*. Twentieth Anniversary Edition, Harper San Francisco, 1999.
Another essential introductory book, *The Spiral Dance* explains how Witchcraft is especially appropriate as a spiritual path for feminists and environmentalists. It is refreshing in that it presents Wicca as a spiritual path, not just a system for casting spells.

Starhawk, Diane Baker, and Anne Hill, *Circle Round: Raising Children in Goddess Traditions*. Bantam Books, 1998.
One of the clearest ways in which Wicca has grown into a mature religion since it first appeared in the public eye 50 years ago has been in the number of resources now available

for raising children according to Pagan belief and practice. Of several books currently available on the topic, this is by far the best. It explains the beauty of Goddess spirituality on a level appropriate for children, and does it so well that it works for adults, too.

Robin Wood, *When, Why ... If: An Ethics Workbook.* **Livingtree Books, 1996.**

If you'd like to know more about the ethics of Paganism and Wicca, this is an excellent resource. Wood, a well-known Pagan artist and designer of a popular Tarot deck, here examines the philosophy of right and wrong as applicable to the old religion.

What are some good Wiccan Websites?

Wicca and other forms of Paganism have a strong presence on the Internet. Countless individual Pagans have created Websites dedicated to their spiritual beliefs, and many covens, groves, and other nature spirituality communities have web pages as well. Plus, a small number of Wiccan/Pagan networking organizations exist, which have created truly professional resources on the Net.

Exploring Paganism online can be a valuable and up-to-the-minute way to be informed about the hard-to-find world of the old religion. For that matter, many of the leaders of the Pagan world are surprisingly accessible online, making it possible for the dedicated student to receive guidance and mentoring from the best teachers in the community. However, the Internet is certainly not foolproof. For every gifted and highly informed teacher and group, you'll also find a variety of Websites ranging from the mediocre to the just plain bad. Yes, there are "Pagan" Websites that are little more than teenaged rants about how awful Christianity is, or how powerful and accomplished a magician the Website owner is, or (this is truly sad) how one particular type of Paganism is so much "better" than all the other varieties. Yes, Pagans are as susceptible as anyone else to egotism and self-righteousness in regard to their own particular stripe of spirituality.

So when you're poking around on the Internet, use the same degree of caution you would use when meeting a new person in the "real" world. In other words, trust your intuition and common sense. If a Website strikes you as arrogant, angry, silly, sarcastic, pompous, or misinformed, chances are, it's a resource not worth spending too much time on. There are plenty of other Websites well worth your time.

To get you started, here are a few sites worth visiting. All of these are created by recognized leaders in the Pagan and Wiccan communities, or are the official Websites of reputable groups. I've also included one general Website (the Ontario Consultants on Religious Tolerance) that nevertheless includes a wealth of helpful Pagan/Wiccan information. Just visiting these sites will introduce you to more information than you'll ever be able to digest, along with countless links to other resources. Happy exploring!

Cherry Hill Seminary *www.cherryhillseminary.org*
Perhaps one of the surest signs that nature spirituality is here to stay is the formation of this school for Pagan clergy. Although most Pagan traditions provide training for their own

spiritual leaders, the rapid growth of the community has created a training gap in which many Wiccans and Pagans need support in reaching their full potential as volunteer clergy. Pagan priests need the same skills in pastoral counseling, administration, financial management, and liturgical (ritual) design that any other ordained minister requires; and just because Pagans don't pay their priests and priestesses doesn't mean the community expects anything less than the best. Cherry Hill is an important step toward providing professional quality training for the leaders of this rapidly expanding community.

Circle Sanctuary *www.circlesanctuary.org*
This is the homepage of one of the Pagan Community's oldest networking organizations, Circle Sanctuary. As of this writing, their Website is more useful as a source of information than a tool for networking, although Circle does publish an annual guidebook to Pagan groups. Of particular interest is the Lady Liberty League, Circle's watchdog organization that monitors attacks to freedom of religion involving practitioners of Pagan religions. Circle Sanctuary is also the publisher of *Circle* magazine, one of the leading Pagan periodicals.

Covenant of the Goddess *www.cog.org*
Although not as large or comprehensive as the Witches' Voice, the Covenant of the Goddess (CoG) Website still includes a number of interesting essays on both historical and contemporary Witchcraft. CoG, incidentally, is the oldest national network of American Witches; the organization maintains high ethical standards about protecting the privacy of its members and so this Website is necessarily limited in the contact information it provides.

Ontario Consultants on Religious Tolerance
www.religioustolerance.org

This isn't a Pagan Website, but rather a resource created and maintained by a Canadian non-profit organization devoted to educating the public on issues related to religious freedom and tolerance. As such, it is a site with plenty of information on nature spirituality, as well as a variety of other religions, both mainstream and alternative. The site refrains from passing judgment on any one path and carefully avoids endorsing one spiritual view over another. The emphasis is on tolerance as a value worth pursuing for its own sake. Of particular interest is an intelligent and balanced article on the question of how many people actually practice Wicca and other forms of Paganism.

PanGaia *www.pangaia.com*

One of the best of the Pagan-oriented magazines, *PanGaia* provides a comprehensive coverage of nature-oriented spirituality, through articles, essays, and reviews. It's a quarterly magazine published by a company that brings out several other magazines of interest to Witches, including *SageWoman* (specifically written from a feminist perspective), *The Blessed Bee* (covering issues of concern to Pagan parents), and their newest venture, *NeWitch* (exploring Witchcraft specifically for young adults).

Proteus Coven *www.draknet.com/proteus/*

I've avoided listing coven Websites in this list because many of them provide information only of interest to the people participating in that particular coven. However, the Proteus Website is a wonderful resource for the entire Pagan community (and beyond). Under the tutelage of High Priestess Judy Harrow, this Website provides an abundance of articles and essays on the philosophy and theology of the craft. It's written from a liberal perspective (liberal even by Wiccan standards), but the information presented is intelligent and balanced.

The Witches Voice *www.witchvox.com*

The Witches' Voice (or "Witchvox") is the best place to begin your search of Wicca and Paganism online. A volunteer Website run by two Florida-based Pagans, it includes regularly updated news stories, editorials, and other articles, and one of the best databases of Pagan contacts to be found anywhere. This list includes individuals, groups, and businesses that cater to the nature spirituality community. It even includes information and resources specifically for teens. It's refreshing to see a Website as large and useful as this one remain so resolutely non-commercial.

Conclusion

Thank you for taking the time to learn about Wicca and nature spirituality. Even if you never attend a Pagan ritual or remain convinced that Witchcraft is something you disagree with, I applaud your open-minded willingness to learn. As a devotee of the Goddess, I do not expect everyone to agree with me or even to approve of my spiritual choices. All I ask for is a world where tolerance, respect, and goodwill can triumph over prejudice, bigotry, and discrimination.

May your life and your spiritual journey (in whatever form it takes) be filled with happiness, love, and joy. Blessed be!

Index

About the Author

Carl McColman is the author of several books, including *The Well-Read Witch*, *The Complete Idiot's Guide to Paganism*, and *Embracing Jesus and the Goddess*. He is a metaphysical teacher and spiritual guide based in Atlanta, Georgia. Visit Carl on the Web at *www.carlmccolman.com*.